From High Heels to Gumboots

One Cow Pie at a Time

June Hilbert

From High Heels to Gumboots

One Cow Pie at a Time

JUNE HILBERT

From High Heels to Gumboots
One Cow Pie at a Time

All rights reserved
Copyright © 2013 by June Hilbert

Reproduction in any manner, in whole or in part,
in English or in other languages, or otherwise
without written permission of the publisher is prohibited.
The publisher can be contacted at jahilbert@mindspring.com

The information in this book is true and complete to the best of my knowledge. The author disclaims any liability in connection with the use of this information.

ISBN-13: 978-1490353067

PRINTED IN THE UNITED STATES OF AMERICA
By CreateSpace.com

About *From High Heels to Gumboots*

Never again will I doubt the power of love—a love so strong it can make a city girl forsake her stylish, high heeled shoes and don the clumpy gumboots of a ranch wife.

In this hilarious, loving and enlightening new book, June Hilbert pulls no punches in explaining why the gumboots were a darn good idea. In a "cow-calf operation," we learn, one might well also find need of a hard-hat, safety goggles, a bottle of liniment, a good "emergency" bottle of wine, and an unfailing sense of humor.

This old city-boy loved it.

—**Max Yoho**, Kansas author and humorist

Readers who have navigated successfully mixed marriages on the farm or ranch—that is, the union of partners from rural and urban upbringings—will identify with June Hilbert in her funny, honest and energetic adventures after joining her country-reared, professional entomologist husband Bill on his cow-calf ranch in northeastern Kansas.

If this marriage was made in Heaven, it was also made with pluck, good faith, determination, humor, intellectual curiosity applied on the go, the usual give-and-take and some amounts of physical courage and willingness to work through the many animal care crises that arise in these operations. Cow pies and placentas form something of a glue here, while Hilbert's frankness about ranch realities wins the reader's trust.

—**Jim Suber,** Veteran agricultural columnist, vegetable grower and county commissioner

This is a hilarious accounting of a city slicker becoming a farm wife. Whether you hail from the city or the country, you'll be able to relate to the bittersweet experiences of life on the farm!

—**Jody Holthaus,** Meadowlark Extension District Agent, Livestock-Natural Resources.

DEDICATIONS

To Bill—a/k/a Technical Consultant
Without you, none of this would have been possible!

To all our cows, past and present
Stepping in your cows pies made me a better person.

To farm and ranch wives everywhere
You have my sincere respect and admiration.

I would also like to acknowledge and thank:

Max and Carol Yoho for their valuable guidance, mentorship, and support.

Table for Eight, my writers' group: They took me in on a cold December evening and provided warmth and sustenance to my muse. Their comments and suggestions have meant the world to me. Plus, they're all a lot fun!

Donna Sullivan and Jody Holthaus, for graciously taking time to read and comment on my manuscript. They provided unique and valuable information and insights from their perspectives.

Morgan Chilson, my editor: Her guidance and suggestions for tightening down the text and amping up the action have made a huge difference. I've learned so much and appreciate her input, advice and especially her enthusiasm.

CONTENTS

INTRODUCTION—MEET THE HILBERTS   1
   June's Story—From Town Girl to City Girl
   Bill's Story—You Can Take the Boy Out of the Country,
      But You Can't Take the Country Out of the Boy
   Our Story

THE FIRST ADVENTURE   11
   Gentle Ben – The Prodigal Steer

BLESSED EVENTS   15
   Please Pass the Whiskey
   Twins Times 2
   Bovine Teenage Pregnancy
   A Backwards Blessing

UNFIT MOTHERS   31
   Chug-A-Lug

MARGINALLY UNFIT MOTHERS   35
   From Search-and-Rescue Mission to Near-Death Experience
   Candy Calf

ADOPTIVE MOTHERS   45
   "It smells like my calf, but it doesn't look like my calf!"
   A Match Made in Bovine Heaven

DISEASE, PESTILENCE AND OTHER BOVINE MALADIES   49
   Peggy Sue
   Prolapse
   One-Toe
   Put Up the Cross and Say a Prayer

"DON'T FENCE ME IN"   57
   Range Cubes and Lifesavers
   Creek of *So Close, Yet so Far*
   Shooting the Gap

BOOMER SOONER BOVINES	63
ATYPICAL DAY ON THE HILBERT FARM	77
FROM PIECE OF CAKE TO PIECE OF COW PIE	83
NON-BOVINE ADVENTURES	93
Snake Slayer	
Gumbo Chicken—A/K/A Attack Rooster	
A WALK ON THE WILD SIDE	99
Dances With Snakes	
Coyotes in the Fog	
In the Timber Primeval	
Alien Cattle Rustlers	
FARM FRESH FILOSOPHIES	105
Hay-Fever—Not Just an Allergy	
MARS AND VENUS ON THE FARM	111
It's a Man Thing	
Pasture Pyrotechnics	
Mars and Venus in the Laundry Room	
Quid Pro Quo on the Farm	
DOMESTICITY ON THE FARM	121
All Work and No Play Makes June a Very Bitchy Girl!	
Feng Shui on the Farm	
Farm Fashion	
I'm Not Having a Hot Flash—We're Burning Hedge!	
FUN AND GAMES ON THE FARM	131
Farm Federation Tag Team Rat Smack-Down	
Cow Pie Frisbee	
Splish-Splashing on the Farm	

CARS, SEX AND COUNTRY ROADS 137

REALLY GROSS FARM AND PET STUFF 143
    Cattle
    Bon Appetit!
    Gross Dead Smelly Stuff
    Skunks

HAUTE CUISINE ON THE FARM—LIVING OFF THE LAND 149
AND THE LAKE
    To Die For...Literally?
    Fashionista at the Fur Harvesters' Supper

REUSE, RECYCLE, REPURPOSE—THE FARMER'S 155
SURVIVAL TRILOGY

BOVINE DATING AND MATING HABITS 157
    Romancing the Cow
    Love Potion No. 9

"EE-I-EE-I-O"—A LITTLE COUNTRY MUSIC 163

WHEN THE LIGHTS GO OUT IN THE COUNTRY 167

OUR GOLDEN GIRLS 173
    Ginger
    Taffy
    Brandy
    Amber
    Cricket

BEYOND THE PAVEMENT 187

I am a
farm wife.

My life begins
where the pavement ends.

INTRODUCTION

Meet the Hilberts

My destiny was sealed by a head of broccoli.

After our first date, my future husband ignored the symbolic bouquet of flowers to appear at my desk with a head of broccoli bigger around than a dinner plate.

My co-workers proclaimed him a "keeper," and three years later, on July 12, 1985, I married a farmer. He may have been forced to make a fulltime living working for the Kansas Department of Agriculture, but Bill was a farmer at heart. He pastured 10 yearling steers on a 10-acre farm west of Valley Falls, Kansas.

And I became a part-time "farm wife."

June's Story:
From Town Girl to City Girl

Prior to 1982, if someone had told me my future was to marry a cattle farmer, I wouldn't have believed such a wild prophesy. In fact, I would have laughed. Me, a farm wife? Remember those captions under the senior class pictures in high school yearbooks: "The boy most likely to...." and "The girl most likely to....?" I would have been a strong contender for "The girl *least* likely to end up as a farm wife." In fact, at my 30-year class reunion, Bill and I regaled some of my classmates with tales of my experiences as a "Certified Bovine Midwife Assistant." One of the gals who had grown up on a farm looked at me incredulously, pointed her finger and exclaimed, *"YOU?!"* See what I mean?

June Hilbert

I grew up in a small rural community, Burlingame, Kansas, a no-stoplight town with a population of 1,000. The closest city, Topeka, was about 30 miles away. We didn't make that trip very often. In those days, we could buy most items we needed in Burlingame or in Osage City, the largest town in the county with a population of 2,000—but no stoplight. Or, there was always mail order from the Sears & Roebuck or Montgomery-Ward catalogs. For the most part, if we couldn't get it in the county or from the catalogs, we probably didn't need it.

My parents were both raised on farms in Osage County. They were young children during the Depression and Dust Bowl; consequently, neither one wanted to make farming their livelihood as adults. After they were married, they lived in Lyndon, the county seat. Both worked for the county: Dad for the road and bridge department and Mom in the abstract office. In 1951, Dad got a job with a plumbing, heating and electrical business in Burlingame so they moved.

Visits to our grandparents' farms were highly anticipated events when my brother, two sisters and I were growing up. We had Sunday family dinners often at both farms. During the summers, we enjoyed longer visits, often several days and nights at a time, at the farms. There was a big barn to play in, timber to explore, farm equipment to climb around on, cute baby chicks to hold. Sometimes Granddad let us sit on his lap and steer the tractor or the 1954 Chevy pickup. Grandma took time out from her chores to push us in the swing. Our swings at home were kid-propelled. Yes, the farms were great places to visit. We even thought living with our grandparents would be paradise—no house chores to do and unlimited access to the cookie jar.

The only farm chore we were allowed to participate in was gathering eggs with Grandma. The cattle were off-limits. We could get kicked or stepped on. I also suspect this had something to do with my sister and our cousin opening a gate and liberating some of Granddad's cattle!

After graduating from high school, I was college-bound. After college...well, beyond that point my future plans were murky. I entered college intending to major in Home Economics. My selection process for choosing a major was more of an elimination process. I knew what I absolutely did *not* want to do. Teaching was at the top of the list. Nursing was close to the top, followed by anything involving business much to my mother's chagrin. She encouraged me to take business courses in high school, advice which went ignored. I was too busy taking college preparatory courses—biology, chemistry, physics, algebra, composition. I wasn't going to be a secretary, for heaven's sake! Basic typing was sufficient for college term papers.

A major in music was another consideration of short duration. I did have a broad musical background: ten years of piano lessons, playing clarinet in high school band, vocal and instrumental accompanist, and some experience playing the organ. A career in music was generally limited to teaching—*not a chance*—or performing—*ditto*.

So, by process of elimination, I'd settled on Home Economics as a career choice.

In 1972, Home Ec was still all about "stitch and stew." Did I like to cook? I told myself I did. Did I like to sew? Heck no! I hated sewing. My mother was an excellent seamstress. Those genetics sailed past me and splashed down in my sisters' gene pools. My preliminary plan was to focus on the food part, take only the required minimum of sewing courses and maybe throw some journalism into the mix. I could write about food for a living.

The fall I entered Kansas State Teachers College at Emporia, Kansas, the school was reinventing its image away from "Teachers College." Over the next couple of years, almost all departments eliminated the mandatory student teaching block for non-education majors. The Home Economics Department was one of the holdouts. As my advisor explained, "Whatever you do in Home Ec, you will always be teaching someone something." *Me, teach?* Teaching was at the top of the list of occupations I considered to be fates worse than death. The mere thought of student teaching scared the beejeepers out of me. Please don't misunderstand—I have the utmost respect for the teaching profession. But I didn't have any confidence, indeed I had grave concerns, about my ability to maintain order and control in a classroom, let alone try to teach the kids anything.

My solution to the problem was to transfer to Kansas State University and enter the dietetics program. The transfer actually solved two problems: no student teaching and no more sewing classes. However, another problem was looming on the horizon. To catch up to the other first semester juniors in my chosen curriculum, my advisor placed me in three science and chemistry lab classes consisting of two courses in the dietetics program and general organic chemistry. *Yikes!* Science and chemistry were not my strong suits. Struggling with a killer class schedule, I worked my butt off that semester, studying any time I wasn't in class. The result? Major burn-out. Heck, I only experienced one party night in Aggieville, the student night life spot. How pitiful is that?!

Truthfully, when I entered Kansas State in the fall, I was having serious reservations about my newly chosen field. I wasn't *excited* about the new direction and my future was still murky; it wouldn't come into focus. My career selection by process of elimination was not working. In a moment of gut honesty, I realized my reason for going to college was because I had been a straight A student throughout high school and assumed it was expected of me. My perception was if I didn't go to college my family and teachers would all be disappointed. Of course, their perception was I had my future under control. Nothing could have been further from the truth!

A self-misdirected career choice. Severe educational burnout. Feeling lost and like I didn't belong anywhere. My screwed up life had evolved into a crisis looking for a place to erupt.

Time to engage the PAUSE button on my life and regroup.

When I arrived home at the end of the semester, my parents decreed I would not be allowed to languish at home while sorting out my life. I had to FAST FORWARD myself out into the world and get a job. "Oh, and while you're at it, get an apartment and a car. You're moving to Topeka." The ultimatum was not as callous as it sounds. They were very supportive during this transition period and even used personal and business connections to help me accomplish the trifecta. Within two weeks, I had landed a job, staked out an apartment and bought a car, thanks to a low-interest loan from The First National Bank of Mom and Dad.

Landing the job was a "right place, right time" stroke of luck and a life changer. A major Midwest savings and loan in downtown Topeka was anticipating an opening for a receptionist/clerical position on the executive floor. The job had not yet been listed. I placed an application for what I assumed would be a teller position. I was offered the receptionist job and ecstatically accepted. So began my life as City Girl. 8-to-5, here I come!

During the next several years, my City Girl persona developed along with my career. I advanced from executive floor receptionist to a departmental administrative assistant. I moved from a one-bedroom apartment to a condominium. City life was shopping at the mall, Friday evening happy hours with friends, dancing at nightclubs, attending movies, plays and concerts, and eating out at restaurants. Yes, the working world and city life suited me just fine.

Then, in 1982, I broadened my horizons by taking up running and joining the local runners club. I volunteered to work at a competitive swim-bike-run event, Topeka Tinman Triathlon. The runners club representative on the triathlon organizing committee gave my name to the event chairman and suggested he contact me in person because, as he put it, "Oh, by the way, she has great legs!" So Bill appeared at my desk one day, introduced himself and asked me to lunch at a later date. He didn't get to see the "great legs"—I was sitting at my desk. But he did see them several days later when he took me to lunch. He must have liked what he saw because he asked me to dinner the evening after the triathlon.

Bill's Story:
You Can Take the Boy Out of the Country, But You Can't Take the Country Out of the Boy

Bill grew up on a farm in western Douglas County, Kansas, which was homesteaded in 1856 by his great-great grandfather Hilbert. The farm passed down through the generations to Bill's dad. Bill was a true farm kid, helping with the cattle, sheep, hogs, chickens, guineas, ducks, geese and rabbits, planting and harvesting crops and putting up hay. He also worked on his uncle's dairy farm during the summers. Life consisted of getting up in the morning and doing chores before going to school, then coming home in the afternoon and doing more chores. It was long hours, hard work and very little money. He and his two sisters had the necessities, but very little else. He has told about receiving one toy at Christmas and being thrilled to death about it. Compare that to kids' Christmas's now!

Like my parents, Bill saw the writing on the barn wall—farming as a livelihood wasn't for him. Neither was working in a factory, like the local Goodyear tire plant. So he set his sights on college. Financially, he would have to pay for it all—no scholarships and no financial help from his parents. It would mean holding down several part-time jobs, but he was no stranger to hard work. So, after high school, he went to Baker University for two years, then transferred to Kansas State University where he majored in entomology, the study of insects.

He graduated from K-State in 1968 and was offered a graduate assistantship at Rutgers University. Unfortunately, he strayed too close to an "Uncle Sam Wants You!" poster. No, he didn't get drafted, but almost. In 1968, at the height of the war in Viet Nam, the President nixed (a subtle clue as to the identity of the President) deferments for grad school students. Bill enlisted in the Army, rather than wait for the Army to find him, hoping he could have some control over his military destiny. The enlistment strategy, along with several other strategies aimed at staying out of Southeast Asian jungles, must have worked. He spent almost three years on a base in Germany in an Army Security Agency unit and gallivanted all over Europe during that stint.

Once he had fulfilled his obligation to Uncle Sam, he enrolled in graduate school at K-State and resumed his education. In December, 1974, he earned his Masters degree in entomology and was hired by the State Department of Agriculture in its plant protection division. He was assigned an area covering 25 counties; and his job entailed inspecting and licensing tree and shrub nurseries and greenhouses, surveying crops for insect and disease infestations, and inspecting export commodities including grain, hay, logs and lumber. He and the job were a perfect fit—he could be outdoors and the venue was mostly rural areas.

Five years later, he bought a ten-acre farm west of Valley Falls, Kansas, then bought six yearling steers to fatten and sell. He was back to farming, but on a small scale and not dependent on it for his livelihood.

Prior to moving to the Valley Falls farm, Bill underwent extensive knee surgery to repair a ligament tear. As part of his post-operative rehabilitation, he started swimming at the Topeka YWCA with a Masters group. Masters swimming is organized fitness and competitive workouts for adults. Triathlons were just catching on as competitive endurance events and the Topeka Tinman was the brainstorm of a Masters post-workout chat session. The local runners club and bikers club as well as other support organizations were invited on board and the event was launched.

The second year of the Tinman, Bill was chairman of the event organizing committee. The runners' club representative, who apparently had ulterior motives of playing Cupid, told Bill about a new girl in the club who wanted to volunteer at the event. Starting to sound familiar? "Oh, by the way, she has great legs!" The result? Farm Boy meets City Girl. Farm Boy dates City Girl. Farm Boy marries City Girl. Farm Boy takes City Girl out of the city.

Our Story

For the next three years after that first dinner date followed by Bill's presentation of the legendary head of broccoli to me at work, I lived my life in the city during the week and spent time in the country on Bill's small farm on weekends. This urban/rural split was a novelty in my life. I headed for the farm after work on Friday, then returned to the city on Sunday evening to prepare for the coming work week. I didn't have to make the 50-minute commute twice a day.

Bill's farming operation was small and low maintenance. By then, he had increased his herd to ten yearling steers which he bought in the spring and sold in late fall. Except for being fed hay in early spring and late fall, the steers were self-sustaining on grass. Bill also kept a few chickens and a clock-challenged rooster that crowed at all hours and for no apparent reason. The farm pets were Ginger, a young Golden Retriever, and Mrs. Gray, a gray-striped cat. I didn't interact much with the steers other than to watch them graze. The chickens held no interest for me, especially since they were not producing more than a few eggs and, therefore, not earning their keep. But Ginger was full of personality and fun to play with. Mrs. Gray and I kept our distance due to my allergy to cats and her doubts about my worthiness to set foot on the farm.

After about two and half years of this part-city/part-country existence, Bill hinted about dropping the city part and making the country part full time. His rationale made sense—I love you; you love me; let's get married. What a romantic devil!

Yes, I loved him and wanted to spend the rest of my life with him. But that meant moving to his farm. Bill had lived on a busy thoroughfare in Topeka for a short time and was adamant he would never again live in the city. Continuing to live in my condo during the week and going to the farm for weekends was not an acceptable option. Bill's country roots ran much deeper than my city roots and I understood that. I was committed to the relationship and our future together, so I started packing.

Those first two years of married life on the farm were a major adjustment. There were adventures. While Bill was away on a trip, one of the steers decided the grass was indeed greener on the other side of the fence ("Gentle Ben" chapter). I killed my first snake ("Snake Slayer"). There were learning experiences: building a fire in a wood stove ("I'm Not Having a Hot Flash—We're Burning Hedge"); surviving without electricity in the aftermath of an ice storm ("When the Lights Go Out in the Country"). There were unexpected hardships: no dishwasher, no air conditioning, only one small bathroom. I'm not a morning person so sharing a bathroom stretches my tolerance dangerously near the breaking point. After a couple of feral snarls, Bill caught on.

Two years later, we started looking for a bigger farm closer to Topeka. We eventually found a 40-acre farm about 20 minutes from my job in downtown Topeka. And get this: the house had a dishwasher, central air and *two* bathrooms. Such luxury! But wait—there's more: two-car attached garage with one automatic garage door opener (mine, of course!) and refrigerator with icemaker.

With the increased acreage, Bill expanded his cattle operation and changed his focus. He started a cow/calf operation with thirteen cows great with calves. My hands-on experience with cattle also expanded. I fed cattle, bottle-fed calves, assisted with difficult births, extradited cattle on the lam back to our side of the fence, became a voyeur of bovine sexual activity and stepped in cow pies, an occupational hazard that goes with the territory.

Bill's work responsibilities occasionally required him to be gone overnight, sometimes for two or three consecutive nights. At this time he was also participating in a male bonding ritual in the form of an annual fishing trip to Canada for ten days. Most of my farm adventures inexplicably occurred when he was gone.

For the next twenty-one years, as the cattle operation continued to expand it quickly outgrew our own land so Bill started renting other pastures in the area. He also accumulated various types of farm equipment including tractors and the equipment they pull, which are necessary to maintain a farm and cattle operation.

Then in 2005, we were offered the opportunity to purchase a 160-acre farm about a mile from our present place. The owners were an older couple who were on a waiting list to move into a retirement facility in Topeka. They didn't have any direct heirs and wanted to sell the place to someone who would be a responsible steward of the land and wouldn't divide it into smaller plots to sell. This farm had been in the man's family since it was homesteaded in 1857 and was the oldest surviving farmstead in the township which had remained in one family. We had known this couple since we moved to the area and had rented the pasture for the past fifteen years.

The farm sat on a hilltop with a panoramic view of the pastures and timber. There was a ranch-style home, a big barn and several outbuildings, all in immaculate condition. Oh yes—there was also an outhouse, in not quite immaculate condition, but I hoped that wouldn't be an issue because there *was* indoor plumbing.

Three years later, the couple moved to their retirement facility and we moved to our new farm. We were ecstatic! We felt like land barons!

By this time, our cow/calf operation had expanded to 60 pair, plus two bulls charged with the responsibility of perpetuating the operation.

Depending on the time of year, the tally might also include part of the yearling heifers and steers from the previous year's calving. The bovine census count could reach as many as 130 to 140 animals, scattered among our own pastures plus the approximately 200 acres of land we rented.

Bill was still employed at his job with the State Department of Agriculture but had been eligible for early retirement for several years. It didn't take long for him to decide settling into the new farm would require more than part-time effort. In March, 2009, he retired and became a full time cattleman.

If you've been doing the math on our moves from one farm to the next, you can see we quadrupled the acreage each time: from 10 acres to 40 to 160. I assure you we will *not* be moving to a 640-acre farm!

Taking the Girl out of the City was the easy part. Taking the City out of the Girl catapulted me right out of my comfort zone and into the world of cow pies!

June Hilbert

THE FIRST ADVENTURE

Gentle Ben—The Prodigal Steer

My first farm adventure was prophetic of many future adventures—a critter on the lam and Bill away from the farm on a work or guy trip.

Bill was a member of a professional organization called Horticultural Inspectors Society (HIS). Each October, the central states division holds a conference in one of the capital cities. The conference convenes on Monday and adjourns Thursday noon. This means for four days, it's just me and the cattle. I swear these animals know this!

In our early years together, Bill's cattle operation consisted of ten yearling steers. He bought them in the spring when the pasture was ready for grazing, fattened them up, then sold them in the fall after at least one hard frost and, hopefully, made a few bucks. Compared to the cattle operation we now have, those were the simple years.

So, one Monday morning in those simple years, Bill went off to the HIS conference. He had intended to sell the steers before he left, but just didn't get around to it. As he explained before he left, "You don't have to do much. Just check on them occasionally and make sure they're all still here." No mention of what to do if they weren't.

Well, as I've learned through the years, I should have seen this one coming. Tuesday morning's count was one short. I recounted—still one short. *OK, now what?*

At the time, I didn't recognize this as the auspicious occasion it was: my inaugural *OK, now what?* moment. Many would follow.

I started walking the fence and quickly found Gentle Ben, a woolly, light brown steer, on the wrong side, chowing down on the neighbor's grass. Another thing I've learned through the years: a critter on the lam usually doesn't wander far from the herd, just to the other side of the fence.

This was Gentle Ben's second escape. The first time, Bill drove him along the fence to a gate and he willingly walked through and rejoined the herd. This time, we were about 100 yards from the gate. He moseyed along the fence until we were within a few yards, then he veered off in another direction. I dashed around to drive him back toward the gate. He veered off in still another direction. Again, I dashed around to drive him to the gate. We repeated this dash-and-drive scenario but were moving farther from the gate. I was going to be seriously late for work!

I left Ben contentedly grazing the greener grass on the other side of the fence and trotted to the house: first, to call a neighbor for help and, second, to call my boss. I didn't know many of the neighbors yet, but had met the one whose property was behind ours. It was a big dairy operation. I was mortally embarrassed to have to make this call, picturing the neighbors laughing their heads off at the green-horn City Girl. But I sucked it up and made the call anyway. The farmer's wife said her husband was out doing chores but would be over as soon as he was finished—about a half hour. My boss was very understanding, encouraging me to do what I needed and not worry about being late. What a great guy!

When the neighbor arrived, we were able to double-team Gentle Ben and get him through the gate—piece of cake!

"He sure is a gentle steer!" remarked the neighbor.

I looked at Ben and thought, "Couldn't you have put up a little token resistance so this guy wouldn't think I'm as useless as tits on a steer!"

I thanked the neighbor profusely and headed for the house to get ready for work. When I arrived around 10:30 my boss rushed out of his office to express his concern for my prodigal steer. I assured him Gentle Ben was now home, and thanked him for being so understanding. He returned to his office. A few minutes later, the elevator doors, located about 20 feet from my desk, opened and a rousing rendition of "Home on the Range" burst forth, sung by a hastily assembled and slightly off-key corporate choir. Word of my predicament had obviously spread throughout the building. My boss—what a great guy!

Bill called that evening to see how I was faring with the cattle. I related the whole adventure to him. He was puzzled why I had so much trouble convincing Gentle Ben to go through the gate when he walked right through for Bill. This experience would set the stage for future adventures: Situations Bill could easily resolve became farm fiascos for me!

When Bill returned home he solemnly vowed that, in the future, any cattle on the property would be sold *before* he went to the HIS conference. Then he emphatically crossed his heart etc. etc.

Remember this for future reference.

Trying to get a few of the previous year's fall calves, ranging in age from eight to 10 months old, organized for a photo shoot. They look so innocent, but the shenanigans start when Bill leaves on a trip!

June Hilbert

BLESSED EVENTS

"The happiest days are when babies come!" Melanie Wilkes exclaimed to Mammy after the birth of Scarlett and Rhett Butler's daughter in *Gone with the Wind*.

"Another healthy calf. Life is good!" is Bill's version of this quote.

My first experience with bovine obstetrics came after we moved from the 10-acre farm near Valley Falls to the 40-acre farm near Meriden. With more grazing acreage, Bill changed his cattle operation from buying yearling steers to fatten and sell, to buying pregnant cows to calve, known as a cow-calf operation.

There was a learning curve to this cow-calf business and for me, it was pretty steep. I knew nothing about bovine labor and delivery. Having never experienced the birth process myself, most of what I knew about human labor and delivery came from coffee breaks at work and baby showers. Those stories made me seriously consider never again having sex! Women who have given birth seem compelled to compete for bragging rights to who endured the longest labor; who popped out the kid in the car/truck/Harley; or at a stoplight/hospital parking lot/elevator; who suffered the most pain without drugs; or who suffered the most pain with drugs. Scary stuff!

But with Bill's tutoring, I learned more about bovine blessed events than I ever thought I would need to know. For instance, I learned to recognize the signs of imminent birth:

Udder Development - Several days prior to delivery, the udder becomes firm, as opposed to its normal jiggly state, as it fills with colostrum. Called "making a bag" or "bagging up" in Farmerese.

Strutting of Teats - The teats also become firm and appear to jut out from the udder at a slight angle, versus hanging limply. "Springing" in Farmerese.

Relaxing and Swelling Around Tailhead and Vulva – This is the area where the calf is expelled from the cow's body. Also referred to as "springing" in Farmerese. By my observation, this area pooches out; hence the June-ism for this stage is "pooching."

Mucus Discharge – A stream of yellowish mucus hangs from the vulval opening. "Stuff" or "Goop" in June-ism.

Isolation - A few hours prior to the birth event, the cow leaves the herd and seeks a remote area of the pasture for privacy. Unlike the current trend in human births, cows do not invite the whole family, including tenth cousins, to participate in the grand event. Nor does she encourage photos to be posted on Facebook. Cows are particularly modest and old-fashioned.

By my own personal observation, I have added a sign that usually occurs at about the same time the udder starts to firm up: dropping. Think about how the baby bulge of a human expectant mother drops a few days prior to birth. I swear an expectant cow mother does the same thing, except the drop is not vertical. It is more of a lateral move of the calf bulge from the lower middle section to the right side near the back end. So far, none of the veterinarians we know will confirm this observation. Another June-ism.

When we start to observe the early signs of an impending blessed event, we become extremely vigilant. No doubt, the cow finds this compulsive attention annoying. At least once or twice a day, someone hunts her down and peers intently at her udder and butt. With all this attention to her tits and ass, she probably thinks we're a couple of perverts. Fortunately, the cow doesn't realize we can actually observe the labor and delivery process through binoculars from our house, depending on her maternity ward site selection.

Generally, cows give birth without human assistance. No Lamaze coach telling them when to breathe and no doctor telling them when to push. Usually, they get along fine with only Mother Nature as midwife. However, just like human births, cows can have complications. In the event of birth complications on our farm, Bill steps in as what I call a Certified Farm Midwife or CFM; I am the CFMA, or Certified Farm Midwife Assistant.

Please Pass the Whiskey

Our first cow-calf herd began with 13 cows Bill bought from a neighbor. They were due to calf in mid to late spring. Our first blessed event was not only my first experience with bovine birthing but also with the human-assisted bovine delivery procedure known as "calf-pulling."

Calf-Pulling 101 - The term used to describe the human-assisted bovine delivery procedure. It is what it sounds like. The farmer midwife literally pulls the calf out of the cow. This is done either by tying a rope around the unborn calf's front hooves which are protruding from the cow, or by using a bovine birth assistance device known as a "calf-puller." By either method, calf-pulling is messy business. The person operating the calf-puller or pulling on the rope stands immediately behind the cow and gets covered with everything that comes out of her rear end. I'm lucky to be the assistant—I stand *behind* that person while we pull.

The first of our 13 cows to give birth was in labor for an unknown amount of time. Bill found her in the pasture lying on the ground, struggling. He could see the calf's feet poking out so he got her up, herded her to the corral and barricaded her in the loading chute. This was in the days before we owned a squeeze chute so, in true farmer fashion, we made do with what we had. She didn't particularly want to be messed with, but was in too much pain to resist.

Bill tied a rope around the ends of the protruding calf hooves and pulled. The calf didn't budge. He called to me to help but even pulling together, we still couldn't dislodge the calf. We didn't want to risk detaching the calf's hooves from its legs, so we quit before we had a real catastrophe, and I was dispatched to the house to call the vet. The receptionist said he was out on a call and couldn't come for almost an hour. I was getting panicky and in a shaky voice told her "By then we'll have a dead calf and probably a dead cow!" She said she would call him and try to get him out as soon as possible.

I raced out to the corral and gave Bill the news—no vet for almost an hour. He sent me back to the house to call the neighbor who sold him the cows and ask if he could come over and bring his calf-puller. No answer. I raced back out to the corral with that news. Meanwhile, the cow was making distressed mooing noises and Bill was still trying to pull the calf. By this time, he was starting to panic. He still won't admit to it, but he was definitely in panic mode. He told me to run back in and call another neighbor, Earl, who he thought might have a calf-puller.

We need to take a break here so I can tell you about Earl. Shortly after we moved to this new farm, Earl showed up one Saturday to welcome Bill to the neighborhood—with a pint of Canadian Club whiskey. He didn't intend to give the pint to Bill; he was already swigging from the bottle and wanted Bill to have a couple of drinks with him. This was how Earl spent some of his Saturday's; he would drive around the area, pull into a driveway, wait for the farmer to come out and have a couple of drinks with him. It was Earl's way of socializing. If the farmer wasn't home or just didn't come out, Earl would leave—no hard feelings. Bill hopped into the truck, had a couple of drinks and talked farming. On a few occasions, Earl came by just as we were leaving. Bill went out to Earl's truck, told him we were leaving, took one swig of Canadian Club and Earl went on his way down the road. He'd come back some other time.

I'm ashamed to admit I considered Earl a pest; I was still harboring traces of City Girl Snob mentality. But Bill predicted someday, Earl would turn out to be a good friend and neighbor to have. The prediction proved to be true as we return to the story of our first blessed event.

I raced to the house to call Earl, hoping he was home and sober. He was home, sounded sober and, yes, he had a calf-puller and would be right over. A few minutes later, he pulled into the drive. He and Bill attached the calf-puller to the cow and pulled the calf with very little effort. We were the proud and relieved god-parents of a huge, black bull calf. No wonder the cow needed an assisted delivery! This blessed event called for celebration! We had an unopened pint of whiskey in a kitchen cupboard. I ran into the house and brought it back to the corral. We opened it and passed it around about three times, swigging from the bottle. From then on, when Earl drove into the yard on Saturday, I went out and greeted him—didn't swig any Canadian Club, but chatted as good neighbors do.

We named the calf Whiskey.

* * *

We had another huge, black bull calf that spring and, fortunately, the cow had a totally natural birth experience. Several days after this calf was born, I was out by the corral watching it nurse. Generally, when calves nurse, they stand to one side of the cow. At this particular meal, the calf was standing between the back legs of the cow. Suddenly, mama had a #2 nature call. The calf jerked out from between the cow's legs but not before taking a direct hit. He looked over at me and he had a big, dark green, icky cow pie oozing down over his head. I was sitting on the top rung of a gate and laughed so hard I nearly fell off. Cow pie happens! I named this calf "Poophead."

Another one of the calves born that spring happened to be a buff color so we named it, appropriately, Buffy. Our Golden Retriever, Ginger, was also buff-colored. I swear Buffy thought Ginger was its sister. Buffy would walk up to Ginger, sniff her, then lick her nose. Ginger would reciprocate and they would continue this kissy-face game until Buffy's mama roared up and ran Ginger off.

Those 13 cows and calves were my first experience with farm blessed events. It was exciting but also very humbling as I gained a new, if somewhat tipsy, appreciation for my neighbors.

Twins Times 2

Once again, on a Monday in mid-October, Bill departed for his annual HIS (Horticultural Inspectors Society) meeting; once again, I was home alone with the herd. (The exciting stuff never happened when the Kansas Chapter hosted the meeting!) Remember the Gentle Ben incident when someone promised that all cattle on the place would be sold before he went to this meeting, cross his heart etc. etc.? Uh huh!

After arriving home from work Monday evening, I changed into farm clothes. Brandy, our Golden Retriever at the time, and I set out on our evening walk in the pasture. The fall calving operation wasn't complete so I had to do a head count to determine whether or not someone might have retreated to the "maternity ward" part of the pasture. We hiked up to a small hilltop to get a better view to count. I summoned the ladies as Bill had taught me: "S'boss, s'boss! Sook, sook, s'boss!" Roughly translated, it means "Come, cow."

I started counting moving targets, "1, 2, 3...19, 20, 21." Darn! One short. Once more, just to be sure: "1, 2, 3...19, 20, 21." Still one short. The hilltop vantage point provided a good panoramic view of the whole pasture except for behind the dam of the back pond, a popular labor and delivery area. I walked to the pond and started around the end of the dam. There was my missing cow, lying down but with her head up and chewing cud. She saw me and struggled to her feet so I quickly left. I felt bad about disturbing her but my suspicions were confirmed: another blessed event was imminent.

Brandy and I walked back to the house and about an hour later, after dark, I grabbed the rechargeable spotlight and ventured out to check on the cow. The trick was to check on her, but not spook her so she left the area, with or without her calf. I hiked up over the hill near the pond, stopped and shined the spotlight toward the labor and delivery area. She was now standing up and I saw two little shiny dots on the ground in front of her. Those shiny dots were the newborn calf's eyes. I slowly edged closer to get a better view. The cow moved and turned toward me. Then I saw another pair

19

of shiny dots. Huh?! Two pairs of shiny dots meant two calves. *Twins?!* Another *OK, now what?* moment.

I cautiously moved a little closer yet. The cow got fidgety and made nervous mooing noises, indicating visiting hours were over and time for me to leave. But not without one last look. One calf was standing by the cow and the other was lying on the ground. Yep—twins!

I hurried back to the house to make phone calls. The first one was to Charlie, a former neighbor, whom Bill asked to come by daily to check on the cows. He stopped by that afternoon and thought the cow was close to calving. On the phone, Charlie assured me he would come by the next morning and check on the cow and calves.

Next, I called Bill, or rather, the hotel where he was staying. He wasn't in his room, which wasn't unusual since the meeting agenda included evening work sessions. The desk clerk asked if I wanted to leave a message. I was still pretty amped about the whole twin thing and blurted out, "Please tell him we had twins!"

The clerk replied, "Twins? Well, congratulations!" Oh, an obvious misunderstanding here.

"No, no. I'm sorry—not me—one of our cows!"

"Ohhhh!"

"Please have Bill call me. Thanks!"

At this point, I tried to recall what Bill had said about twins. The only thing that came to mind was a concern the cow would not realize both calves were hers, so she would reject one, abandoning it to become coyote bait. It's not like you can tell her, "Congrats, Mom, you have twins!" Great! I might be bottle-feeding a calf.

Another major concern: for a calf to survive, it must either suckle from the cow or be bottle-fed a colostrum substitute within 12 hours of birth. The substitute provides antibodies critical for building immunities. My anxiety meter was about to redline!

Bill finally called after 9 p.m. This was a first for him and he was excited. He also wanted more information. Would I go back out and, without spooking the cow, try to determine whether or not the she had cleaned off both calves. (The post-natal cleaning off is like a human newborn's first bath to cleanse off the birth slime. The difference is the cow uses her tongue. It reminds me of when Mom used to clean my face with spit on a hanky.) If both had been "bathed," it was a good indication the cow accepted them as hers. So, how would I know if she cleaned off both of them? By this time, they should look dry. If one was still wet and slimy-looking, it still had birth gunk on it; therefore, it had not been cleaned and, in all likelihood, was rejected by the cow.

I threw on my farm coat, grabbed the slowly-dimming spotlight and a pair of binoculars. One more trip schlepping any more gear out there and I would need a backpack. Oh, did I mention the maternity ward was in a back corner of the pasture, as far away from the house as possible? A one-way trip was about a half-mile. Let's see...how many times tonight had I trekked out there?

So, back to the maternity ward one more time. The plan: creep as close as possible, then turn on the spotlight and use binoculars to see if both calves had received their first tongue-bath. Surprisingly, the spotlight didn't seem to spook the cow. She just didn't approve of me getting close. I crept forward until I heard the cow softly moo, cow-speak for, "That's close enough." I set the spotlight on the ground and focused the binoculars. The calves were lying down. Were they both dry? I couldn't be absolutely certain but at least they looked the same, which wasn't shiny, so I optimistically decided "yes." Whew!

Gathering up my gear, I headed for the house. The phone was ringing as I walked in the back door. It was, of course, Bill. Yes, both calves looked dry. Yes, I would check on them in the morning before leaving for work. Yes, I called Charlie. Yes, I love you too. Goodnight.

I was exhausted from all the excitement and numerous trips to the pasture, but since my anxiety level was still elevated, I poured a glass of wine. Later, as I drifted off to sleep, an image popped into my head. It was of Bill handing out cigars at the HIS meeting.

I awoke the next morning to the sound of rain pounding on the roof. Great! I dragged myself out of bed, dressed, hunted down rain gear and ventured out into the semi-darkness and driving rain to take Brandy for her morning run and check on the new family.

Mama and the twins were still behind the back pond. One calf was nursing, the other was lying on the ground with its head up so I knew it was alive. Making a mental note to call Charlie and give him the update, I slogged through the pouring rain back to the house and a hot, steamy shower.

As I reluctantly stepped out of the shower, the phone rang. Yes, it was the proud new godfather. I answered the barrage of questions, some of which were reruns from last night, then, after reminding me to call Charlie, Bill signed off, "I love you and I'll call you tonight."

Coffee! I needed coffee! Lots of coffee!

The next concern was whether or not both calves would get enough to eat from Mama. Charlie made daily trips to check on them. Each morning, I got up early and went out to check when I took Brandy for her morning exercise. Then I checked again in the evening. On each trip, I would attempt to get close enough to the new family to make sure both calves were suckling. Unfortunately, I was a little too obsessive. By moving in too close, I spooked the cow so she would walk away and take the calf suckling with her, leaving the other one lying on the ground. It didn't seem to want to get up and follow. I assumed it was not getting enough to eat so was weak and, therefore, would starve to death. In a semi-panic, I consulted Charlie. He assured me he had not only seen both calves suckling, but they were up and walking around. I asked him if we should take the abandoned calf to the barn and pen it up so I could bottle-feed it. He advised me to give it another day. Intervention could cause more problems than it solved if it wasn't necessary in the first place. If the cow thought we were taking her baby away, she could get agitated. I agreed, somewhat reluctantly, with Charlie's wait-and-see advice.

Bill arrived home—*finally!*—late Thursday afternoon. We walked to the pasture to see the new family and check the rest of the herd. As we approached the cow and twins, one calf jumped up and skipped closer to Mama. The other one got up slowly and just stood there. It didn't seem to have the energy level of its twin, an indication it wasn't getting as much to eat.

I named him "Reject." Bill named the other twin "Repeat."

The following Sunday was Halloween. Bill was keeping tabs on another cow about to calve. When he checked on her Sunday morning she had admitted herself into the maternity ward. He looked at her again a couple of hours later and, lo and behold, we had another set of twins! Two sets in a week's time are unusual with a herd of only 22 cows. We named those calves "Trick" and "Treat."

In the following weeks, it became apparent the mothers of the two sets of twins didn't have enough milk to sustain an acceptable weight gain on both calves. The probable future result: one twin would show a below average gain, and the other would gain even less. Time to cut the financial loss. The smallest twin of each set, Reject and Treat, would be sold as bucket calves so the two remaining calves, Repeat and Trick, could have all the milk and a better chance for typical weight gain.

Bucket Calf 101 – A calf raised as an orphan so it must be hand-fed formula milk. The container used is a bucket with a nipple inserted in the side near the bottom rim, or a large bottle with a nipple.

Sadly, the choice was all about dollars and cents. With an operation as small as ours, we couldn't afford to give in to sentimentality. Reject and Treat were sold to a neighbor who had the time and resources to bottle-feed them until they were big enough to be pastured.

My introduction into the world of bovine twindom had all the elements I was coming to expect in my part-time farm wife internship: absentee farmer husband; *OK, now what?* moment; helpful neighbors who provided valuable support and bailed me out when necessary; barrage of questions from absentee husband requiring innumerable trips back and forth to the pasture to answer; late night glass of wine to relax me followed by early morning cup of coffee to kick me into gear. But most important are the memories of my adventure with our first set of twins, Reject and Repeat, and of the Halloween twins, Trick and Treat.

Bovine Teenage Pregnancy

One April evening Bill, Brandy, and I headed out to the pasture for our daily walk. We passed by the corral where we had 20 heifers penned up waiting to be released into the pasture, along with a bull, so they could be bred for the first time.

A word here about first-calf heifers, i.e., new mothers. This can be a dicey undertaking for the inexperienced cattleman because:

1. First-calf heifers do not read *What to Expect When You're Expecting*. You just hope the new mother has the instincts to guide her through the process.

2. They do not attend baby showers and hear about the birth experience war stories of the other mothers. Come to think of it, that's probably fortunate.

3. They do not attend pre-natal classes and you cannot give them pre-natal advice. It's all up to God and Her midwife, Mother Nature.

As we passed by the corral, we saw one of the heifers lying on her side, flat on the ground, struggling. "Oh no! She's having a calf!" was Bill's shocked analysis of the scene. When he fed them earlier in the day, this heifer was off by herself, a sign she might not feel well. But going into labor?

To be calving now would mean she was only four or five months old when she was bred. That's like a pre-teen! Not likely, but it was happening! Our first first-calf heifer was about to give birth.

We launched into crisis mode. Not knowing when the actual labor had begun but fearing it had gone on for several hours, Bill coaxed the heifer to her feet and herded her into a chute so he could pull the calf. We still didn't own a set of calf-pullers, but Bill had a fence stretcher that worked on the same principle. He wrapped a small chain around the calf's protruding front hooves, attached the other end of the chain to one end of the fence stretcher rope and tied the other end of the rope to a fence post. He started pulling the lever of the ratchet. (Note: If you are reading this and pregnant, you might want to skip ahead. What comes next could give you nightmares for the duration of your pregnancy!)

Bill worked for what seemed hours, but was actually only a few minutes. The heifer was becoming weaker from the prolonged labor and delivery stress. Bill, generally optimistic by nature, feared he was delivering a dead calf. He regrouped and worked the ratchet one more time. Out popped the calf's head and front legs. One more pull and the body was halfway out. One final pull and the calf was on the ground. But was it alive? Bill shook it gently—no movement. He checked the nose for breathing but couldn't feel any breath. He picked up a piece of straw and tickled inside its nose. The calf snorted, opened its eyes and squeaked out a pitiful little bawl. It tried to lift its head but flopped back on the ground. It was alive, but just barely. It needed nourishment, STAT.

I raced to the house, mixed up a bag of just-add-water colostrum substitute in a feeding bottle, then raced back to the corral. Bill lifted the calf's head and worked the nipple into its mouth. The poor little thing was so weak it didn't have the strength to suck. Trying to pour even a small amount of the liquid down its throat could result in choking.

The only hope was a feeding tube inserted through the mouth and down to the stomach, but we didn't have one. In desperation, Bill called a neighbor. Yes, he had a tube and would be right over. Thank God for country neighbors!

The neighbor arrived, inserted the feeding tube into the calf's mouth, threaded it down the throat to the stomach and administered a portion of the vital nourishment. He left the feeding tube with Bill with instructions to wait a few hours, then try to get the rest of the colostrum mixture into the calf. Around midnight, Bill reheated the mixture, gathered his equipment and headed to the corral, wondering if he would find a live or dead calf. The calf was alive and the feeding was a success.

By the next day, the calf was able to make wobbly attempts to stand. Bill tried to guide the calf to the mother so it could suckle, but nothing happened. Our new teen mother sniffed at the calf but didn't seem to know what to do with it. So Bill started bottle-feeding milk replacer, or baby calf formula, twice a day. During the second day, Bill tried again to guide the calf up to a teat, but still, nothing happened. Then, on the morning of the third

Weaning calves is cause for separation anxiety! Bill uses "fence line weaning" so cows and calves can still touch noses and see each other. Studies indicate this weaning process creates less stress than total separation.

day, Bill went out to the corral with the bottle of milk replacer and there stood our new young mother with her calf sucking away on a teat, wagging its tail—a sure sign it was getting groceries. Oh, happy day!

I lost count of the number of times Bill remarked, "That calf is lucky to be alive!" Appropriately, he named the calf "Lucky." As for our teenage mother, I named her "Jailbait!"

Jailbait became another pet. She loved range cubes (cow treats) and ate them out of our hands; she followed us all over the pasture when we went out to check cows with Lucky trotting along beside her.

Some months later, when Bill weaned the calves born to our older cows, he included Lucky. It was time for the next phase of a calf's life cycle and Jailbait did not take it well. Her separation anxiety went beyond the usual two to three days of bawling and searching for her calf. I knew something was terribly wrong when she quit eating range cubes out of my hand. I approached her with my arm extended and a cube in my hand but she backed off, then turned and walked away. It was like I was to blame for taking away her calf. Bill got the same reaction.

In our cow-calf operation, the life cycle progression was:
1. Cow has calf;
2. Cow gets bred again in two to three months while still nursing calf;
3. Calf is weaned at seven to eight months;
4. Process repeats.

So, by the time Lucky was weaned, Jailbait was due to calve again in two to three months.

This may sound overly dramatic, but I believe Jailbait's separation anxiety escalated into depression. There was a definite personality change and she just wasn't the same Jailbait. Later that fall, Bill sold her along with some other bred heifers due to calve in early spring. Our operation was based on fall calving and she didn't fit the cycle.

At the risk of extending the over-dramatization, I have to admit I felt a god-motherly sort of bond with Jailbait and Lucky: the "teen mother," the desperate struggle to deliver and save the calf, the joy and relief when new mother and baby finally figured out how mealtime worked, and feeding Jailbait range cubes by hand, then having her follow me around begging for more.

As I think about Jailbait, I wonder how she fared at her second birthing.

A Backwards Blessing

Like a human newborn, a baby calf comes into the world head first or, more specifically, nose first. Unlike the human newborn, the calf's front hooves also come out with the head. Any other position is cause for alarm and means either a call to the vet or herding the cow to the barn so Bill can attempt to pull the calf.

In our first experience with abnormal birth position, Bill had been monitoring a cow in hard labor for about an hour. Once he realized she was having difficulty delivering her calf, he herded her to the barn and put her in the chute. When he looked at the pelvic opening and saw the nose and only one forefoot, he knew the other leg was bent back. The vet wasn't available so he called a neighbor who had experience in repositioning a bent leg.

From High Heels to Gumboots

The neighbor arrived, put on a shoulder-length plastic glove and sleeve, reached into the birth canal and felt around until he found the bent foreleg. He pushed the calf back into the birth canal—not easy to do since the natural inclination of the cow was to push it *out* of the canal—and turned the calf until he could reposition the bent leg. He was then able to pull both legs forward until the hooves were visible. He and Bill attached the calf-puller and delivered the calf. Sadly, it was dead. Too much time had elapsed from when the water bag broke until the delivery.

A few years later, the same situation occurred late one evening with another cow in prolonged delivery effort: nose showing and only one hoof visible. While Bill herded the cow to the barn I called the vet. Yes, he could be here in about a half hour, around 9:00. The vet arrived, repositioned the foreleg and pulled the calf. Once it was on the ground, he tickled its nose, hoping it would snort out any mucus blocking its airway. He couldn't coax out a snort but it blinked, then shallow little breaths whispered from its nose. Bill released the cow from the chute, she trotted to her calf and started licking it. We all backed off to let the mama perform her post-natal bonding ministrations. After awhile, the calf lifted its head and uttered a weak bawl. The vet left and we went to the house. Bill went out an hour later to check on the pair. The calf was up and greedily sucking down its first meal.

A year later, Bill found another cow struggling to deliver. This time two hooves were visible but no nose. He herded the cow to the barn then rushed to the house to get his "CFMA" (Certified Farm Midwife Assistant)—me. I grabbed a pair of heavy work gloves and raced to the barn. (Notice how I seem to "race" everywhere? Twelve years as a competitive runner have served me well in farm crises.)

"CFM" (Certified Farm Midwife) Bill assembled his bovine assisted-delivery instruments, using an overturned stock tank next to the squeeze chute as an instrument table. The patient was restrained in the chute.

"Glove," Bill demanded as the delivery procedure began. Notice I didn't mention scrubbing up—we don't.

I handed him the long plastic glove from the instrument table. He worked it on over his hand and work shirt sleeve. (We don't wear surgical scrubs, either.) He reached into the birth canal and performed an exploratory examination.

"I was afraid of that," he muttered. "The calf's backwards."

"Hand me that small chain," he directed. "Now hand me the calf puller." He fastened one end of the chain around the hooves and the other end to the calf puller. He hooked the calf puller to a post. Then he sat on the ground, braced his feet against the end of the chute, gripped the rope and started pulling in unison with the contractions of the cow. In bovine delivery, the cow determines when to push and the CFM takes his lead from her. However, the CFMA was mentally coaching her to push.

The first push/pull didn't budge the calf. Bill rebraced his feet and regripped the rope. "It'll be a miracle if this calf's alive," he muttered between clenched teeth. By now, he was sweating profusely so I grabbed a rag off the instrument table, reached into the chute and wiped his forehead. I didn't know where he got the rag or if it was clean and didn't want to think about it.

The cow bellowed as she bore down with the next contraction. Bill grunted as he powered through the pull, leaning back until he was almost flat on the ground. Suddenly, the legs and butt of the calf squeezed out. Bill levered himself up, pulling hand over hand until he was sitting upright again. One final, mighty pull and the calf slid out and down to the ground.

I looked intently at the calf, willing it to show some sign of life. I heard a soft gurgling noise and thought its midsection raised very slightly, an indication of shallow breathing. "The calf is alive!" I whispered excitedly.

Bill grabbed some grass and tickled its nose to make it snort. Then he picked it up by its hind legs and gently shook it to dislodge mucus in its airway. He laid it back on the ground and it continued to breathe shallowly. By now, the cow was bawling and fighting to get out of the chute. Bill sent me out of the corral and released her. She charged out of the chute, circled around to her calf and began licking it.

The calf was barely alive and would be too weak to suck, either from the cow or a bottle. By then, Bill owned a feeding tube but had experienced disastrous results when he used it, losing a calf. If the tube isn't properly inserted and goes into the lungs instead of the stomach, the calf dies. Feeding too much too soon will also result in death. So Bill called the vet's office. The vet was working several horses and wouldn't be able to leave for some time. But, Bill could load up the calf and take it to the clinic and the vet would tube it.

Bill prepared a bag of colostrum substitute, poured it into the feeding tube, loaded the calf in the back of his pickup and went to the clinic. He returned over an hour later with the live calf and instructions on how to tube feed, for future reference.

Three hours later, Bill checked on the pair. The calf was sleeping and the cow stood watch over it. He picked up the calf and tried to get it to stand, only to discover its front hooves were bent under. Having previous experience with baby bovine orthopedics, Bill went to his medical supply cupboard and found narrow, flat pieces of wood to use as splints, and duct tape. He taped the little splints to the calf's legs. The calf was still too weak to suck so Bill put the cow in the chute, milked her out and tube-fed it to the calf.

The next morning, Bill milked the cow again. This time, the calf took the bottle. That evening, when Bill checked on the pair, prepared to again milk the cow, the calf was standing at the cow's udder, slightly wobbly, sucking on a teat. Yet another success story on the Hilbert farm!

Bill named this calf Lucky-Peg, for two of its predecessors: Lucky, for the calf of the teen-age mother, Jailbait, and Peg, for Peggy Sue, another calf born with deformed hooves who spent several days in the rigged-together splints.

June Hilbert

UNFIT MOTHERS

Sadly, unfit mothers exist in the bovine world just as in the human world. It happens with cows that have birthed several calves as well as first-calf heifers. At least with first-calf heifers, it's easier to understand: new mother didn't know what to do or there was a communication breakdown with Mother Nature. With older, more experienced cows, it becomes a puzzle. Did the cow take one sniff at the calf and decide it was ugly and she didn't like it? Did she decide she was sick and tired of the whole motherhood gig? She might want to reconsider because if a cow doesn't produce calves, she doesn't have a purpose and therefore doesn't have value. She transfers to the liability side of the farm ledger sheet and is doomed to become hamburger.

So far, we've only had one instance of total calf rejection by a cow with previous calving experience.

Chug-A-Lug

Cow #58 rejected motherhood for the life of a party girl. Apparently, she decided she fulfilled her motherhood obligation by popping out the calf. Once that feat was accomplished, she wasted no time returning to her friends and a free-and-easy lifestyle of grazing, cud-chewing, gossiping with the girls, carousing around the pasture and flirting with the neighbor's bull. During the first days after the calf was born, Bill would find it alone, either sleeping or bawling for its mother. He would go after the cow, herd it to the calf and put the calf up to a teat so it could eat. Good cow mothers stay close to their calves for the first few days. Not Party Girl!

Finally, Bill herded both cow and calf to the barn for some quality bonding time in a pen. Hopefully, the maternal instinct would kick in. Didn't happen. Somehow, Party Girl jumped over a five-foot-tall fence panel to rejoin her friends not once, but twice. The odd part was most of her friends had calves, but she didn't seem to notice.

Because of Party Girl's disinterest and abandonment of her offspring, we had a poor little rejected foster calf to feed. Twice a day Bill mixed up calf formula with warm water and put it in a two-quart plastic bottle with a big nipple. The little foster calf sucked it right down. Yum!

Bill was officiating high school football and volleyball that fall so when he had games scheduled, I stepped in as Foster Mother. I remembered from past baby-sitting experiences letting babies eat too fast without burping resulted in the milk coming right back up. Not knowing how a calf's digestive system worked, I considered only briefly trying to throw him over my shoulder to burp him. The next thought was to make him take a break occasionally by taking the bottle away. He tried to reach for it. I put it out of sight behind my back. He trotted behind me. I lifted it up out of reach. He looked up at the bottle, looked back down at me, grabbed a mouthful of my jeans leg and started sucking! I gave the bottle back to him. After feeding, I went back to the house with several slobbery wet spots on my jeans.

I named this calf "Chug-A-Lug!"

Mid-October rolled around. Yes—that time again. Bill went off to the HIS meeting and I was left back at the farm to deal with whatever chaos was in store for me. This particular year it meant I was in charge of feeding Chug-A-Lug both breakfast and supper. Supper wasn't so bad, but hauling myself out of bed at 0'dark-thirty was a killer! I'm not a morning person and, as far as I know, I was born this way and will remain this way until the day I die. (Note to funeral planner: Please schedule my funeral service for afternoon.)

Prior to leaving for his meeting, Bill expanded Chug-a-Lug's menu to include a grain mixture. Just as human babies progress to cereal, so do bovine babies. Since Gerber didn't make calf cereal, Bill bought a grain mixture of ground up corn, oats and molasses at the feed store. We kept a little tub of this "cereal" in the calf's pen and topped it off as needed.

So, my morning chore schedule went something like this: Alarm went off at 0'dark-thirty, hauled myself out of bed, threw on farm chore duds, mixed up calf formula, grabbed the rechargeable spotlight and headed for the barn. Chug-A-Lug met me at the gate, impatiently bawling for breakfast like he hadn't eaten for days. I stuck the bottle in his mouth and let him chug about a pint. Then I took the bottle away and grabbed a handful of cereal from the tub. Meanwhile, Chug-A-Lug grabbed a mouthful of jeans. I disengaged his sucking mouth from my jeans and stuck my handful of cereal in it. Luckily, my hands are small so I could stick my whole hand in his mouth, palm up, then draw it out slowly, letting his top gum scrape the cereal off my palm. Force-feeding was necessary because he really didn't want cereal; he wanted milk! After forcing a few handfuls of cereal into him I let him wash it down with another shot of milk. We repeated this ordeal, including the jeans sucking, until all the milk was gone.

With Chug-A-Lug fed, it was on to the rest of my morning farm chores: take our dog, Amber, out to the pasture to do her business; and check the cows for any more newborns. Please, no babies this week! Chores completed, I dashed back to the house to shower, style my hair while gulping coffee, eat breakfast while skimming the paper to see if anyone I knew was hatched, matched, dispatched or snatched, take Amber to the barn, throw on "dress for success" business suit, swipe on a dollop of makeup, and head out to work—a 20-minute drive into the city. I was already exhausted and this was only the first day!

On Thursday, Bill returned home from his meeting (hallelujah!) and resumed most of the foster parenting. By then, Chug-A-Lug had become such a pet Bill let him out of the pen for short periods. Bill opened the gate, Chug-A-Lug trotted out and followed him to the house. While Bill was in the kitchen whipping up calf formula, Chug-A-Lug stood in the garage and bawled for his meal. One morning, a neighbor on her way to work stopped by, came to the back door and asked, "Do you know there's a calf in your garage?" Bill replied, "Oh yeah. That's Chug-A-Lug waiting for his breakfast."

When Chug-A-Lug was out of his pen, Amber enjoyed her new playmate. They sniffed noses and chased each other around the yard.

Even though the whole experience sounds like an ordeal—and it was!—it was also fun. Chug-A-Lug was such a little character. I still chuckle to myself when I think of him trotting around me trying to find the bottle, then grabbing a mouthful of my jeans!

A few more weeks passed and Chug-A-Lug gained enough weight so Bill could take him to the sale barn. We both had demanding full-time jobs so it wasn't feasible for us to continue the feedings through the winter. I was sad to see him go, but I knew he would make a great 4-H project calf for someone.

And what was Party Girl's fate? The menu at McDonald's!

June Hilbert

MARGINALLY UNFIT MOTHERS

Unlike Unfit Mothers, some cows don't fully abandon their calves, but display an indifferent attitude, as if to say, "If the calf wants to eat, *it* can find *me* at mealtime. Then, get lost, kid, I'm busy chewing cud!" I have designated these cows as "Marginally Unfit Mothers."

From Search-and-Rescue Mission to Near-Death Experience

On a Friday evening in late September, Bill was officiating a high school football game, leaving our Golden Retriever, Cricket, and me to do the usual evening walk around the farm to check on cattle. As we were ambling along the path through the timber, Cricket suddenly stopped, perked up her ears, raced down the path as if she were in hot pursuit of something, then came to an abrupt halt. I caught up with her and found a little black pile on the ground. A small head slowly lifted out of the little pile and a mournful, squeaky sound came from its mouth. Cricket had found a baby calf just a few hours old. A visual check of the calf showed it had been cleaned off—no birth slime and its hair was dry. Assuming the new mama was close by, I looked around the area, fully expecting her to come charging in to protect her baby. After a few minutes and no sign of the mama, I tried my best imitation of a calf bawl. Still no mama, but the calf bawled back at me. A good mother would not wander far from her newborn calf. However, we had a few first-calf heifers that year and abandonment can be an issue with new mamas. I was facing yet another one of my *OK, now what?* moments.

I stayed with the abandoned calf for awhile but no mama came to claim it. The calf attempted to stand but collapsed back into a little pile on the ground. Dusk would soon turn to darkness and darkness would bring chilly air and predators. The calf needed quality nourishment in the form of colostrum, the real stuff or the replacement variety, and protection.

Murphy's Law of the Farm: Anything that can go wrong will go wrong when Bill is gone. He wasn't due home for several hours, *if* he didn't stop at a "watering hole" to quaff a brew and rehash games with other football officials. No time for hand-wringing! I had a calf to save from starvation and protect from predators.

As we hurried back to the house, I formulated my strategic rescue operation:

1. Contact Bill to make sure he came straight home from his game; no stopping for a post-game brew. He carried two cell phones in his pickup: a state-issued phone and a cheap personal one. Bill is not tethered to his cell phones so gut feeling told me he wouldn't check either one. But I left messages, just in case.

2. Feed Cricket and take her to her house (an old chicken house with no chickens in residence). Newborn calves are usually afraid of dogs; and if, by some chance, the mama did show up, she would take a dim view of having a dog around her calf, if she had any motherly protectiveness at all.

3. Mix up bottle of colostrum substitute, and gather up my jacket, a rechargeable spotlight, a bottle of water and an apple (my supper).

4. Leave a note on the kitchen counter mapping out my location. If necessary I would stay with the calf until Bill found us, hopefully before morning.

I loaded the survival and rescue gear in our Suzuki mini-truck and roared off to the area where we found the calf. But the calf was gone. My rescue mission just escalated to search-and-rescue. After searching the area with the spotlight for a few minutes, I found the calf partway down a creek bank, lying against a bush. Still no sign of the mama.

The search phase of the mission was now accomplished; time to mobilize the rescue phase. After moving the truck to direct the headlights toward the creek bank, I grabbed the feeding bottle and walked down to the calf. Crouched on the ground in front of it, I tried to pry open its mouth to insert the nipple. The calf turned its head and bawled. I tried again—same refusal. I squirted some of the mixture on my fingers and stuck them in its mouth, hoping if it got a taste it would reconsider. Another refusal.

Suddenly, a loud bellow blasted through the air directly above my head! Terrified, I jumped up, scaring the calf who bawled again. Mama had arrived on the scene, shaking her head and bellowing cow-speak for "Don't mess with my baby!"

Mama's arrival and her threatening demeanor were positive signs she possessed maternal instincts at some level. I lifted the calf to its feet and half-carried, half-pushed it up the bank and over the edge toward Mama and the supper table. The calf reached for a teat but the cow shoved it away with her hind leg. I guided the calf back to the udder. The cow again shoved it away, knocking it to the ground. Then the cow walked over to the calf, sniffed and began to lick it. Another good motherly sign, even if she wouldn't feed it.

Now I was faced with deciding whether or not to stay with the cow and calf until Bill found us, or go back to the house. The calf obviously belonged to this cow even though she wouldn't let it eat. My presence only made Mama nervous, so I went back to the house.

Bill arrived home around 10:45 and no, he didn't stop at the watering hole. We drove through the timber to the spot where I left the cow and calf. The calf was there but Mama was not. Bill tried to get the calf to take the bottle but it refused. Then, we heard a crashing noise and Mama lumbered out of the timber toward us, fussing all the way. We backed away from the calf. She walked over to it and assumed a protective stance: head slightly lowered, eyes wary, muscles tensed to deal with these interlopers should the need arise. Bill cautiously guided the calf to the cow's udder but, once again, the cow shoved it away. Bill concluded the calf was apparently getting some groceries from Mama or it wouldn't refuse the bottle. The cow may have pushed the calf away because her teats were sore. Since the cow was showing some protective motherly instincts, Bill decided to leave them alone for the night and check in the morning. He identified the cow as one of his first-calf heifers, #25. We went back to the house, drank a glass of wine and went to bed.

With everyone bedded down for the night, I'll digress and take this opportunity to explain why some cows and calves are referred to by names and others by numbers. In the early, simple years when we ran only a few head of cattle, thinking up names was fun and the names were easy to remember. Also with only a few cows and calves, it wasn't necessary to put numbered tags in calves' ears shortly after birth to match them up with their mothers. However, as the herd increased, we had to start using ear tags. Ear tags are ID bling for cattle—bling-bling if an animal has tags in both ears. The tags are pierced into the newborn calf's ear using a tool similar to the one used when humans have their ears pierced, except the pointed backer is shot through the ear. Piercing causes very little pain and is over in a couple of seconds, as long as the calf doesn't squirm and bawl, "Hey, Ma, somebody's messin' with me!" causing the cow to charge the piercer.

We still name some cows and calves when there is a distinguishing feature or incident that inspires our creativity.

The next morning Bill found the calf alone again in the same area but Mama #25 was nearby. Mama continued to refuse to let the calf suck and the calf continued to refuse the bottle. The only solution was to get the pair to the barn so he could try to milk out the cow by hand. Herding them was not an option; the calf was too weak to make the trip and the cow was uncooperative. So, he enlisted my help. I drove the mini-truck *very slowly* while Bill sat on the back end, holding the calf and doing his bawling-calf impression. Mama followed behind the truck, muttering some low-level cow-cussing.

The distance to the barn was about three-quarters of a mile and the temperature on that late September Saturday morning was climbing into the 80's. The trip took about half an hour, and Mama's mood escalated from moderately irritated to downright annoyed. She was hot and thirsty. Her udder and teats ached. Less than 24 hours ago, her heifer body had painfully expelled some strange little black creature with which she felt some connection but wasn't quite sure what to do about it. Now, some idiot was riding in the back of a truck, holding *her* little black creature, making ridiculous noises and she was compelled to follow by some force of nature she couldn't comprehend.

Our little entourage finally arrived at the barn. Bill shut up the pair in the corral. In her current cranky mood #25 wasn't going to tolerate anyone messing with her teats so she would have to be restrained. The best method of restraint was a squeeze chute. Unfortunately, both of our chutes were among those items still needing to be moved from the farm we had vacated three months previously. But, that farm was only about a mile away and one of the chutes had a hitch and wheels. It was purchased from a friend prior to the move, but Bill hadn't used it yet. He took off in his pickup to get it.

Squeeze Chute 101: A squeeze chute is a cage constructed of tubular steel with front and back gates controlled by levers. The width of the chute can be sized to accommodate any animal from a small calf to a large bull. The principle of the squeeze chute is the cow enters at the rear, and a lever releases a panel that drops down to prevent her from backing out. At the front end, there are two vertical panels that open at an angle toward the inside of the chute. As the cow walks through the chute toward the front, her shoulders push these panels forward and they close loosely around her neck. Now she is secured and can be milked, given shots or whatever else needs to be done.

Bill returned with the squeeze chute and parked it just inside the barn, out of the hot sun. The next project was to construct a pen and alleyway out of cattle panels that funneled toward the chute. This barn, newly constructed and not yet complete, was to be the cattle-working barn but, so far, only the shell was in place. Bill was still working full-time for the State Department of Agriculture and, due to budget cuts, had been putting in long hours. He hadn't designed or built the interior or exterior pens necessary to work cattle. As a result, he was unprepared for this emergency.

Finally, almost two hours after we arrived at the barn with Pair #25, the alleyway and squeeze chute were in place. Bill herded the cow toward the narrowing alleyway. She approached it suspiciously, then turned and trotted back to the far side of the corral. Bill herded her back into the alleyway toward the chute and, once again, she bolted. She shook her head at him and kicked up the cow-cussing a notch, explicitly stating she was nearing the end of her patience with this whole ordeal.

Time for Plan B: Put the calf just outside the front end of the chute as bait to lure Mama in. Bill could then close the rear panel and when Mama's shoulders pushed against the front gates, they would close, stopping her from going on through. Of course, the calf couldn't be expected to stand still so someone—me—had to sit on the ground and hold it. Theoretically, it might work. But I had an odd sort of gut feeling there was something about Plan B that could go very, very wrong.

I sat on the ground just outside the front end of the chute and held the calf. Bill herded the still-cussing cow around once more. As she approached the chute, the calf bawled. Her head jerked up and she saw me messing with her calf. That was the last straw! She lowered her head, angrily pawed the ground, roared out a bellow of pure rage and charged into the chute. What happened next took about one-half second: *CLANG!* Bill dropped down the back panel. I expected to hear the next *CLANG* of the front panels closing around her neck no more than a moment later. It never came. As the realization of impending disaster hit, I looked up into the face of a ballistic, 1300-pound roaring, snorting, snot-slinging cow!

I threw myself to one side, the bawling calf lurched the other direction and the rampaging cow thundered between us! She was on a collision course with the steel barn wall but veered left and lost steam as she circled around the inside of the barn, then trotted back to her calf.

I wasn't trampled. I wasn't dead. I wasn't even maimed for life. But I *was* heart-jack-hammering, adrenalin-flash-flooding terrified! And once realization set in that I wasn't trampled, dead or maimed for life, the terror metamorphosed into *righteously furious!*

Meanwhile, a panic-stricken Bill raced around the chute shouting, "ARE YOU HURT?!"

Was I *hurt?! No,* I wasn't *hurt!* But I *was* lying in the dirt on the barn floor, covered with globs of cow snot and sweating enough to overflow a small stock tank. However much I wanted to jump up and explode, "*What in bloody blazes happened?"* I couldn't and wouldn't. He was as terrified as I was; I could see it in his eyes. Well, maybe not *as* terrified. After all, *he* wasn't the one who nearly bought it under the hooves of a ballistic cow! Having known and loved this man for over 25 years, I knew his fright would manifest itself as anger at himself for putting me in danger. It just never occurred to him anything could go wrong. Intuitively, I knew his anger was about to spew forth and, even though the spewing would only last a couple of minutes and wasn't directed at me, I wasn't yet fully recovered enough to deal with it. I needed to retreat to my Woman Cave in the house and let Bill recover in his Man Cave in the barn.

So I got up, attempted to dust myself off only to come up with a hand slimed with dirt, cow snot and baby calf poop. Only then did it occur to me to check the status of my underpants. *Dry!* I answered Bill's question with a shaky, "No, I'm not hurt."

"I'm sorry. I don't know what happened. You'd better go to the house and clean up." His voice was now deceptively calm, yet had a terse edge to it. Yep, he was communicating to me he needed serious Man Cave time to deal with what had just happened, and what *could* have happened, but didn't. So I plodded to the house accompanied by thoughts of changing my will. This was actually a good sign: my internal pressure cooker was finally letting off the pent-up steam.

Bill worked on the squeeze chute and eventually succeeded in herding the cow back into the chute. He milked about a quart out of her and bottle-fed it to the calf. He kept the pair in a pen at the barn for a couple of days to make sure the calf was getting enough to eat and, if not, to supplement with milk replacer. At the end of that time, he turned them out to pasture with the rest of the herd.

From High Heels to Gumboots

Mama #25 was a "Marginally Unfit Mother." She would feed her calf, but she wasn't very "motherly." She frequently wandered off to another part of the pasture, leaving it alone. When it wanted to eat, it had to find her. As a result, the calf didn't gain weight like its peers. Occasionally, one of the other calves would invite him over for supper. Most of the mamas were not receptive to the idea and some were downright rude, shoving the hungry little calf away from the table.

Mama #25's continued membership in the Hilbert cow/calf operation was looking pretty grim. Bill planned to keep her long enough to be bred again and after the current calf was weaned, Mama #25 was on his "fire sale" list. His plan was to sell cows that fit into one or more of the following categories:

1. An unfit, or marginally unfit, mother;
2. A cow with an insufficient milk supply;
3. A geriatric cow, approximately 12-plus years old;
4. A high-headed bitch (translation: attitude problem).

However, he relented and gave Mama #25 one more chance the next year and she redeemed herself by presenting us with a bouncing baby bull of which she was truly proud. She was a model of bovine motherhood! As Bill said, "She got over her first-calf jitters." The following year, she calved another bull, this one larger than the previous year's. My near-death experience turned out to be one of our best success stories, especially since I lived to tell about it.

Cow standing watch over her calf. A model of bovine motherhood, unlike Unfit or Marginally Unfit Mothers.

41

Squeeze Chute Epilogue: Bill called the friend who sold him the chute and asked about the near-fatal malfunction. The friend's answer? "Oh yeah. Sometimes it does that." *Good grief!* Bill sold that death trap, and his other chute, and bought a new one.

Note to Bill: Thanks for being such a good sport about being "thrown under the tractor" in this chapter.

Candy Calf

Sometimes Marginally Unfit Mothers can be pulled back from the brink of unfit motherhood by a method I termed "coerced bonding": shutting them up together in a pen. We already know this doesn't work with a totally Unfit Mother, i.e., Party Girl. Bill resorted to this method with two first-calf heifers.

During our ritual evening walk, we found a day-old calf, #62, at the back of our property, trying to dart through the barbed wire fence to our neighbor's pasture. The neighbor's cows and calves were grazing just a few yards from the fence. The rest of our herd, including Mama #62, had grazed its way to another area of our pasture. The calf had likely been napping and Mama joined the grazing migration instead of staying with her calf. When the calf woke up it was alone and hungry, and the nearest meal was on the other side of the fence.

Bill sent me to the house to get his pickup. When I returned, he loaded the calf in the back and we set off to find its mother. Once we located her, Bill unloaded the calf and guided it to her teats. The calf latched on but Mama kicked it away. He pushed the calf back to the teats and, again, Mama kicked it away. This apparent maternal disconnect indicated it was time for an intervention in the form of coerced bonding.

We loaded the calf back into the pickup. I got behind the wheel and drove slowly to the barn while Bill herded Mama #62 behind the truck. We arrived at the barn and put the pair into a pen. This cow had a gentle nature so Bill milked her without using a squeeze chute. Then he bottle-fed the milk to the calf. Over the next couple of days, the cow continued to reject her calf. Bill tried distracting the cow by feeding her grain while he guided the calf to her teats. She would let it suck for a short time and then push it away. At this point, coerced bonding wasn't working, Mama #62 was on the brink of Unfit Motherhood, and we had a foster calf to feed.

While Bill was struggling with the Pair #62 family reconciliation, another cow, #13, had her calf but, unfortunately, no motherly instincts. So another dysfunctional family took up residence in the coerced bonding pen. Morning and evening for several days, Bill fed both cows grain, held each calf up its mother's udder as long as she would tolerate, then fed the calves milk replacer to round out the meal. Finally, Mama #13 started to respond. In fact, she responded so well she let both her calf and #62 suckle.

Mama #62 still wasn't catching on to the feeding gig. Then, whether through divine intervention or the desperate longing of the little calf to have a mother of her own, our about-to-be foster calf figured out she could eat at Mama's table from between the hind legs, instead of from the side, and not get kicked. Mama not only tolerated this table arrangement, she finally started to show interest in her calf. After a couple more days, Bill turned both pair back out to pasture.

But the fragile family bond didn't last. The next evening, Bill found Mama #62 in the barn, waiting at the feed tub for grain. Her calf was at the back fence a half mile away, and had resumed its plea to be adopted by the neighbor's cows. Once again, the calf was loaded into the back of the pickup for the ride to the barn and another attempt at coerced bonding.

If the bonding didn't happen this time, we were down to the last option: bottle-feed the calf to get its weight up, then take it to the sale barn and sell it as a "bucket calf" to be hand-fed by a new owner. Mama #62 would be bred again and sold as a second-calf bred heifer. Let her be someone else's problem.

Then we caught a break. Or, I should say, Bill caught a break. Sometimes, he's just so lucky it defies comprehension. Maybe it isn't luck; maybe he's being divinely rewarded for his extreme tenacity. Anyway, someone told him about a product formulated specifically for first-calf heifers and their calves to promote the bonding experience. The product is a granular concoction described as a flavored lick for cattle. The key ingredients are dried molasses and salt, with a little anise oil thrown in. Cows go nuts over molasses, and they crave salt. I don't know about the anise oil. Maybe it's the "cherry on top of the sundae." The granules are sprinkled over the dampened calf and the sweet molasses smell attracts the cow to lick it. Once the "candy" is licked off, the cow gets down to the calf smell and will instinctively recognize and associate it as hers.

Bill bought a container of the product. He sponged a little water over the calf's back, sprinkled the granules on it, pushed it underneath Mama's nose and waited for the magic bond that would epoxy this fractured family relationship. The cow sniffed the calf once, then again, and gave it a test lick. She repeated the sniff-sniff-lick exploration. Her bovine body language indicated something was different here but she wasn't quite sure about it. The product directions didn't guarantee a "Super Glue" type of bonding experience, so Bill left the pair alone for the night. After all, even epoxy needs to set for several hours to form a firm bond.

For the next couple of days, Bill reapplied the granules to the calf twice a day when he fed grain to the cow, and discontinued the milk replacer supplement. He could see evidence of licking because the calf was a sticky mess and smelled like double-shot molasses cookies with anisette liqueur icing. One evening he stood back and watched the cow finish her grain ration and then lick the calf for dessert. He decided it was time to withhold the bait candy to test the strength of the bond. After a couple more days, Mama #62 was still licking the calf even though the candy was gone; the calf was getting regular meals. Bill turned the pair back out to pasture.

Mama #62 remained somewhat inattentive, leaving the little calf with the responsibility of seeking her out at mealtime. But the tenuous bond held.

Bill made another exception to his "fire sale" rule concerning Marginally Unfit Mothers and kept #62 to see how she responded to her second calf. She did not disappoint. For the next several years, she turned out to be one of the best cows in the herd. So good, in fact, two of her daughters were retained as replacement heifers. A "replacement heifer" is a heifer brought into the herd to replace a culled cow, a/k/a hamburger cow, on our farm.

Coerced bonding, sweetened with molasses, pulled Mama #62 back from the brink of Unfit Motherhood.

ADOPTIVE MOTHERS

Running a cow-calf operation has a tragic side; sometimes baby calves die. Even worse, sometimes both the cow and the calf die during the birthing process. Fortunately, we haven't lost any cows, but we have lost calves. Our losses have been minimal because Bill is an attentive cattleman. During high calving season, the cows we pasture at home are checked at least once a day and usually twice for signs of impending delivery. Cows on the rented pastures in our immediate neighborhood are also checked daily.

Regardless of how attentive we are, tragedy still happens. But, Bill is eternally optimistic, extremely resourceful and just plain doesn't like to lose—at anything.

"It smells like my calf, but it doesn't look like my calf!"

The year Bill retired from his job at the State Department of Agriculture, we had 81 pregnant cows due to have fall calves. One morning in mid-September, Bill drove over to one of the rental pastures to check cows. He found cow #9, and a barely-alive newborn calf. Apparently, the labor and delivery had been long and stressful. He loaded the calf into his pickup and took it to the vet. The vet inserted a feeding tube and administered an electrolyte solution. He advised Bill to try to give it colostrum substitute when he got it home. The calf was so weak Bill had to hold its mouth around the nipple of the bottle. The calf didn't take much and, within minutes, was dead. So he now had a dead calf and a cow that historically had been a good mother with a plentiful supply of milk. What a waste!

But wait...he had an idea.

Bill recalled that one of our neighbors, Ray, had a brother who operated a dairy north of Topeka and raised Holstein cows. On a dairy farm heifers rule, bulls drool; they are second-class citizens. This dairyman contracted with a buyer to pick up the baby bulls immediately after birth. (Do bull calves on dairy farms experience teat-envy?) Bill contacted the dairyman, explained his predicament and his idea. The dairyman said he had pulled a huge bull the previous night and, since the buyer had not picked it up, Bill was welcome to come over and look at it. Operation Adoption was launched.

Bill dug into his deer hunting equipment and located his skinning knife. He skinned the pelt off the dead calf, then cut two holes in each end of the pelt and ran twine through the holes. He threw the prospective adoptee's new outfit in the back of the pickup and headed off to pick up Ray and visit Ray's brother.

They arrived at the dairy and checked out the newborn. It was indeed *huge.* But, Bill didn't have any other options at the moment, so he purchased the Holstein calf complete with a money-back guarantee if his plan didn't work out. Since the calf was only a few hours old and still weak from the birthing ordeal, it rode home behind the front seats of our Ford F-150 extended-cab pickup. This method of transport had huge potential to become a smelly disaster. Fortunately, except for one episode of ripe baby calf flatulence, the trip home was uneventful.

Bill and Ray took the Holstein calf to the pasture and tied the pelt around it. The dead calf had been small, about 50 pounds, and the Holstein weighed over a 100 pounds, so the pelt would only reach across its back and part way down both sides. Nevertheless, he put the calf with the bereaved mother. She sniffed it, backed up a step and looked at it, then leaned in and sniffed it again, as if to say, "It smells like my calf, but it doesn't look like my calf!" Not only was the Holstein much larger than her calf, but her calf had been all black and this one was white with black splotches peeking out from beneath the adoptive disguise. Holstein cattle look like Rorschach inkblot tests with legs.

Bill put the calf up to the cow's udder to eat, but when it grabbed a teat, the cow pushed it away. He tried again and she refused it again. He decided to leave them alone for some quality bonding time.

Early in the evening, he drove back to the pasture to check on the adoption status. He took the stock trailer, prepared to load the cow and calf and bring them home if the adoption was not progressing. If the calf had not sucked, the cow would have to be milked to relieve pressure on her udder. When he arrived, the calf was alone. He found the cow, loaded them both in the trailer and came home. He put the cow in the squeeze chute and milked about a quart out of her, then poured the milk into the calf bottle, added milk replacer and fed the calf.

The next morning Bill mixed up another bottle for the calf. When he went out to the corral to feed it, cow and calf were together and mama was licking the calf—a hopeful sign. Bill approached with a bucket of grain for mama and the bottle for the calf. Mama did some cautionary mooing and closely supervised Bill while he fed. The evening feeding was more of the same. The adoption process was headed in a positive direction.

The following morning when Bill went to the corral, the calf was having breakfast at mama's table, making greedy sucking noises and wagging his tail. Sometime during the night, the pelt had come off. Operation Adoption was a success!

This Holstein calf was indeed huge. Ray's comment was, "He's so big, you ought to name him Hoss!" So we did. His full name was Ray Hoss Hilbert: Ray, after our helpful neighbor, and Hoss, since the calf reminded us all of Hoss Cartwright from the old TV western *Bonanza*.

A Match Made in Bovine Heaven

A week later, tragedy struck again: another dead calf, apparently the result of a long, difficult labor and delivery during the night.

Bill was scheduled to be in Manhattan that day. On the way, he stopped at the St. Marys livestock sale barn to inquire whether there would be any orphaned bull calves in the auction that day. There was one black bull calf, so Bill left a bid and continued on to Manhattan. After his meeting, he called the sale barn and the clerk confirmed he had the winning bid. Once again, the method of transport was behind the seat of the pickup. Fortunately, he had the foresight to throw in some old plastic shower curtains and tablecloths to line the floor behind the front seats, because this little calf emitted more than just ripe farts! Later, the plastic shower curtains and tablecloths were hosed off to be used another day. Farm people never throw away these items.

As before, Bill had skinned the pelt off the dead calf to use as a deceptive scent disguise on the adoptee. He tied the pelt on the calf and introduced it to its new mama. This was a match made in bovine heaven!

The cow sniffed the calf, then started licking. The calf found its way to the food source and started sucking. Another success story!

Bill named this adoptive calf Spike. In Farmerese, spiking is the process of substituting an adoptive live calf for a dead one.

DISEASE, PESTILENCE AND OTHER BOVINE MALADIES

Peggy Sue

    Peggy Sue was a fall calf born in mid-April, the product of a neighbor's horny bull jumping a fence and impregnating one of our cows during her first cycle after having a baby calf. Bill had not been expecting any calves so didn't find the cow and calf for several hours after the birth, when his head count came up one short. When he found the pair, Mama was nudging the calf and softly moo-muring, trying to get the calf to its feet so it could eat. Bill eased up to the calf and lifted it to its feet. When he let go the calf fell down, so he lifted it again. He looked down at its front hooves and saw why it couldn't stand: both hooves were turned backwards at the ankle joint.
    Bill had experienced this deformity previously with a couple of baby calves. But only one hoof was affected and, after he performed some gentle massage and stretching, the leg muscles relaxed, allowing the hoof to align properly. But this situation was compounded by both hooves being turned back so the calf was unable to stand and could not get critical nourishment and fluids from the cow. It was weak and dehydrated.
    Bill gently massaged and stretched the deformed hooves but was unable to relax the muscles enough for the calf to stand. Time for a trip to the barn to deal first with the food issue, then treat the hoof deformity.
    Bill transported the calf to the barn in the back of the mini-truck with the cow following close behind. He got part of a bottle of colostrum substitute

into it, then started working on the deformed hooves. But amateur physical therapy wouldn't work this time, so he searched for materials to make splints. Finding a couple of scraps of lath, he duct-taped those to the calf's lower legs, then lifted it to its feet. It was too weak to stand on its own so Bill laid it back down and left it to rest.

He went back out a short while later and fed the rest of the bottle of colostrum to the calf and tried once again to get it to stand. It struggled to take a couple of shaky steps so Bill laid it back down. The bull had passed on a genetic factor that hampered this whole process: longer than average legs. A few excess inches of leg were an added obstacle to getting this calf to walk.

The next day Bill tried again to get the calf to stand and walk a few steps to the cow to eat. It was still too weak to stand for the amount of time necessary to get proper nourishment. Bill started it on milk replacer. He also milked out the cow to relieve the building pressure on her udder and teats, and fed the milk to the calf.

The calf started to recognize Bill as "mama" and bawled when it saw him coming with the bottle. Over the next few days, it gained enough strength to stand and walk with the splints. When it could navigate reasonably well, Bill transitioned it from the bottle to the real mama. A couple of days later, he removed the splints; and, after a few awkward steps, the calf was able to walk. It soon gained enough leg strength to trot along beside mama as normal calves do.

If the calf had been a bull, it would have been named Pegleg. But since it was a heifer, Bill named it Peggy. I added Sue so she became Peggy Sue.

Prolapse

Prolapse 101 - Uterine prolapse in a cow is entirely different from human uterine prolapse. In the human female, the uterus falls, or prolapses, into the vaginal canal when the supporting pelvic muscles and connective tissue become weak. The bovine version occurs either during calf delivery or when the afterbirth is expelled. The uterus is towed through the birth canal with either the calf or the afterbirth.

It's like throwing out the baby with the bathwater, then tossing out the bathtub, too.

One of our cows had delivered her calf in the timber around mid-day on a Sunday. When Bill went out to check on her that evening, he found her and the calf by the pond. The cow was standing and appeared to be in the process of expelling the afterbirth. As he walked closer, he saw a large, red mass hanging out of the vaginal opening. That mass was more than just afterbirth—it was the uterus.

Fortunately, the cow was one of the more amiable ones and Bill was able to herd her and the calf to the corral, a distance of about a quarter mile, the expelled uterus swaying back and forth with each step. He didn't have any experience dealing with uterine prolapse so he called the vet.

The vet arrived that night about 9:00. They maneuvered the cow into the squeeze chute. Bill found an empty feed sack to put the slippery uterus on so he could hold it while the vet stuffed it back into the vaginal cavity. The opening was then stitched up to keep the uterus from falling out.

Once the stuff-and-stitch part of the procedure was complete, the vet went home. Bill left the cow in the squeeze chute while he went to the house to get a syringe and antibiotic to give her to prevent infection. While he was gone the cow peed, making the floor of the chute slick. Then, because she was weak from the delivery and ordeal of the prolapsed uterus, she fell and couldn't get up.

Bill fired up his Bobcat, a small tractor-like earthmover with a dump bucket. He made a sling by running a large log chain around the cow's torso behind her front legs and then hooked both ends of the chain to the dump bucket on the Bobcat. He slowly raised the dump bucket, lifting the cow to her feet so she could walk out.

Once she cleared the chute, she took about five steps and collapsed to the ground, where she remained for the night. Bill put hay and water near her. Since she was unable to feed her calf, Bill fed it milk replacer. From this point on, we referred to the cow as "Prolapse."

The next day Prolapse was able to stand for a few minutes at a time to feed her calf. Bill continued to bottle feed it for a couple of days until Prolapse regained enough strength to provide full meals. After ten days, Bill removed the stitches, then turned the pair back out to pasture.

Having one uterine prolapse does not make a cow more susceptible to future prolapses, as long as the uterus was quickly and properly cared for. However, because of the trauma, possible infection and recovery time, the cow may take longer to breed again or may not breed at all for the next year's calf. With this in mind, once the calf was weaned, Bill sold Prolapse as a kill cow or, as we refer to it, a hamburger cow.

June Hilbert

One-Toe

Foot Rot 101—A hoof infection that occurs when the skin between the two toes on a hoof is either punctured due to injury or softened by prolonged contact with moisture, such as during a rainy spell. Bacteria invade the hoof area and, if left untreated, can result in lameness and poor weight gain due to the animal's immobility. The bacterial infection can also spread to other animals in the area.

We have had a few minor instances of foot rot in our cattle, but most were easily treated with an antibiotic injection that cleared it up in a few days. However, one occurrence got away from us.

Bill bought some bred heifers and turned them out on one of the rental pastures. During late July and early August, he was busy with his job and putting up hay so didn't check on them for a week. They weren't due to calve until around Labor Day so he wasn't particularly concerned. When he got to the pasture, one of the heifers was limply badly, favoring one hind leg. He looked her over and couldn't see any sign of an injury so he assumed it was foot rot. He came home, hitched up the stock trailer, went back to the pasture, loaded her up and brought her home. He gave her an antibiotic injection and took her back to the pasture.

Bill checked a couple of days later and the heifer was lying on the ground and didn't want to get up. He coaxed her up but she could hardly walk. Time for a trip to the vet. The vet treated her with a different antibiotic. Two days passed and the heifer wasn't getting better. The options were limited: amputate the toe and hope the infection did not spread to the other toe, or just put her down. Selling her as a hamburger cow wasn't an option because of a withholding requirement by law for antibiotic treatment. Amputation, of course, would cost money. However, the potential loss from putting down a cow carrying a calf was greater. So Bill played the odds and opted for amputation.

The surgery went well and after a day of observation at the vet clinic, the heifer was released to be brought home. Bill put her in the corral and fed her grain and hay, and filled a small stock tank with water. We were scheduled to leave on a 10-day vacation to Colorado in a few days. We already had a house-sitter hired who could do chores; the vet agreed to make a couple of barn-calls to change the dressing while we were gone. So we headed to Colorado.

While on vacation, Bill called home a few times and everything was going fine.

We returned home on a Friday. On Saturday, Bill attended a volleyball officials' clinic, a requirement to officiate scholastic volleyball. I was home doing the post-vacation umpteen loads of laundry. On one trip from the clothesline to the house, I detoured by the corral to check on the heifer. She had a mucusy, bloody-looking substance hanging from her rear end. *Oh no!* She was having, or maybe losing, her calf. Then I looked at the ground in front of her. Correction: she'd *had* her calf and it was alive. What I saw being expelled was the afterbirth. She wasn't due to calve until around Labor Day so the calf was over two weeks premature. And it was tiny, less than half the size of a normal newborn calf.

Bill pulled into the driveway a couple of hours later, and I rushed out to tell him about our preemie. He was flabbergasted and rushed out to the corral. He had never seen such a small calf alive. He lifted the calf to its feet and guided it over to Mama so it could eat. The calf was so small it couldn't reach the faucets. Bill mixed up a bag of the colostrum substitute and the calf took part of it. Late in the evening, he was able to get the rest of it into the calf and also fed it an electrolyte mixture. He estimated the calf weighed about 35 pounds. A normal newborn calf weighed between 65 and 80 pounds. Even carried to full term, this calf would likely have been below average birth weight because the heifer's partial lameness prevented her from grazing to sustain both her and the unborn calf, and the added stress of the toe amputation.

Bill fed milk replacer to the calf for the next couple of days. Then, on the evening of the third day, he headed out to the corral with the bottle of milk replacer and found the calf reaching up as far as it could, standing almost on the tippy toes of its hooves, with the end of a teat in its mouth, sucking away. Another hallelujah moment on the Hilbert farm!

The calf wasn't yet strong enough to get all its nourishment from Mama, so Bill continued supplementing with milk replacer for a few days. Mama regained her strength and her hoof healed, enabling her to limp along on a hind leg with only one toe. Appropriately, Bill named her One-Toe and he named the calf Itty Bitty.

Several years later, we still have One-Toe. She no longer limps and she raises great calves.

Put up the Cross and Say a Prayer

Losing a calf is sad, but especially when we struggle so valiantly to keep it alive.

During recent fall calving, two of our cows, #15 and #57, dried up—quit giving milk. #15's calf was about three weeks old when Bill noticed it appeared small and thin, compared to other calves born about the same time. He watched it suckle. A happy calf getting enough groceries will suck quite a while from one teat and then move on to another, tail wagging. A calf not getting enough will suck one teat for a few seconds, then move on to another, then another and another with no tail wagging. The latter is what Bill observed. We would have to move the cow and calf to the barn so we could bottle-feed milk replacer to the calf.

Since Mama #15 did not have the gentlest nature, trying to herd her and the calf to the barn was out of the question. We used the method of transport from the chapter on "Marginally Unfit Mothers": I drove the mini-truck very slowly while Bill sat in the bed, held the calf and performed his calf-bawl impression. Mama followed along, tossing her head and making those angry mooing noises, a cow-speak version of "@#%*#!" The trip was fairly uneventful except when we passed by another cow and her newborn calf. Mama #15 let out an angry bellow and roared up to the pair, thinking the other calf was hers. Bill grabbed #15 calf, jumped out of the truck bed and ran over to Mama as fast as he could carrying a 50-pound calf, and made imitation calf bawling noises. She smelled her own calf and followed Bill back to the truck. We finally arrived at the corral without further incident.

Bill tried to give the calf milk replacer and, at first, he shied away. Once Bill got the nipple close to his mouth and he got a taste, he sucked it right down. From then on, someone showing up with a bottle was the highlight of his day. I commented to Bill, "It looks like we have another Chug-A-Lug!" Bill nicknamed him "Chuggie."

About a week later, Bill found another scrawny calf, sucking away on its mama, apparently to no avail. He would make a quick round of the faucets and there was no tail-wagging. This pair, #57's, happened to be standing near a gate into the corral area so Bill opened the gate and they walked through. Calf #57 didn't take to the milk replacer like Chuggie. A few swallows and he was right back at Mama's table. Bill concluded she was producing some milk, but not nearly enough to sustain a calf, much less put any weight on it.

Twice a day, Bill struggled to get milk replacer into Calf #57. Seldom would it take more than a pint. By comparison, Chuggie would chug down two quarts and beg for more. One evening Bill was scheduled to officiate a football game, so I pulled feeding duty. #57 took about a pint and then went back to Mama. I let him suck for a few minutes, then pulled his head around and stuck the bottle in his mouth. He sucked for a few seconds and then turned back to Mama. After another few minutes I pulled his head around, opened his mouth and inserted the nipple. We continued like this until most of the quart was gone, about a 30-minute ordeal. Chuggie polished off his own bottle, then drained #57's bottle for dessert.

After about ten days, #57 was not showing any improvement. One evening as we passed by the corral on our walk, Bill remarked the calf was hanging its head, a symptom of not feeling well. He planned to give it an antibiotic shot in the morning and see if that helped. Sadly, the next morning the calf was dead.

Bill turned Cow #57 and Pair #15 out into a pasture close to the house because we still had to feed Chuggie and wanted to keep him nearby. Cow #57 spent the next couple of days near the corral, bawling for her calf. I was already sad about losing the calf, especially since we fought so hard to keep it alive. But listening to #57's mournful bawl just ripped out my heart.

Puzzled as to why a first-calf heifer and a cow with only her third calf had both dried up, Bill consulted the vet. Cessation of lactation can be an issue with older cows, so he suspected there was an underlying problem with #15 and #57. He needed to know so he could determine what to do with the two cows.

The vet offered several possible scenarios and suggested Bill bring in the cows for testing. Lab results from blood work revealed both tested positive for bovine leukosis virus. Even though only four to five percent of cases that test positive develop into clinical leukosis, there was already an indication, lack of milk, of advancement to disease stage. Tumors will develop in various internal organs and a biopsy can confirm presence of the disease. Leukosis is contagious and can be spread by biting insects, particularly horse flies. The eventual result to the affected animal is death.

Bill knew what he had to do: sell the cows as kill cows, since the disease can't be passed on to humans through the meat, and sell Chuggie as a bucket calf. The likelihood the virus passed to him was very minimal. He would make a good 4-H project calf for some kid.

June Hilbert

"DON'T FENCE ME IN"*

I am convinced there is a Patron Saint of Barbed Wire Fences—St. Barb. Incur her wrath and risk shredded clothes, lacerated skin and cattle wandering all over the countryside. (Note to self: check status of tetanus shot.)

We have a shrine to St. Barb in one of our flowerbeds: a barbed wire ball. It's currently 26 inches tall and 90 inches around. The size of the shrine will increase as Bill has time to wrap more barbed wire around it. I pay homage to St. Barb, asking her blessing on our fences that they may have the strength to keep our cattle where they belong. But, if I fail to show the proper reverence, she'll get even.

Range Cubes and *Lifesavers*

My first solo experience reuniting a cow and calf on opposite sides of the fence occurred in the early days of the cow/calf operation. Ginger, our Golden, and I set out on our evening walk. Bill was gone—of course!—but would be home around 10:00. The pasture was divided into halves by a barbed wire fence with a gate near one end. The cows and calves were in the back half. As we walked through the front half, I heard a frantic high-pitched calf bawl and an answering bawl a couple of octaves lower. As we neared the gate, I followed the direction of the sound to my left and saw a calf running back and forth along the fence on our side about a hundred yards away from the gate; the cow paced back and forth on the opposite side. I identified the pair as Midnight and her calf, Stormy.

Yet another *OK, now what?* moment.

I knew that walking toward Stormy would spook her, and she would turn and run away from me; so I slowly circled wide to the left to get behind her and attempt to herd her toward the gate. She stopped running back and forth along the fence and watched me approach. As I worked around behind her, I made slow shooing motions with my arms. She took a couple of steps toward the gate, then veered to the right and ran off. Meanwhile, Midnight paced faster and bawled louder, obviously unhappy someone was messing with her calf and she was unable to do anything about it.

Since I couldn't herd the calf to the cow, I would have to herd the cow to the calf, and hopefully return both to the back half of the pasture. I climbed through the fence and circled around Midnight to herd her along the fence to the gate. She veered away, circled around me and returned to her spot at the fence. Stormy came back to the fence and resumed bawling. Again, I approached Midnight with gentle shooing motions, but she wasn't leaving her calf.

Time to regroup. Herding wasn't working. I hated to leave the problem for Bill to deal with since he would be home late. Yet I didn't want to create any more anxiety for Midnight and Stormy. Plus, if left to work out the reuniting logistics on their own, one of them might try to go through or over the barbed wire fence, resulting in injury. What kind of farm wife was I if I couldn't resolve a simple problem like this one?!

My fragile self-worth as a farm wife was plummeting. Where's an epiphany when you need one? I turned and began my walk of shame back to the house.

As I passed by the barn, something caught my eye: feed sacks. Some of those feed sacks contained range cubes, a protein and vitamin pellet for adult cattle. In the bovine world, range cubes are candy. Bill shook range cubes in a plastic bucket to train cattle to follow him, instead of trying to herd them where he wanted them to go. Kind of a Pied Piper philosophy but instead of playing a flute, he rattled range cubes in a bucket. (Faced with an emergency situation without range cubes, he has used rocks in a plastic bucket. But once the cattle are located where he wants them, there is no reward. Not something you want to try very often!)

So here was my epiphany. Those range cubes were candy for Midnight, and *Lifesavers* for me! I found a small bucket, threw in a couple handfuls of cubes and headed back out to the pasture.

Snack time! Bill is feeding range cubes to the cows.

My plan was to coax Midnight to follow me toward the gate, a distance of about a hundred yards, and hope Stormy would also follow on her side of the fence. Then I would open the gate and Stormy could run through to Mama. In the event Midnight got through the gate first, I would lure her back with her calf.

I slowly approached Midnight, gently shaking the bucket of range cubes. She immediately stopped pacing and focused her attention on me. She took a few hesitant steps toward me; I again shook the bucket. She took a few more steps then stopped and looked back at her calf. I moved closer and held out the bucket so she could get a whiff of the range cubes. She sniffed but looked back at her calf. The bovine body language communicated indecision...candy or calf?

I grabbed a range cube, leaned toward her and waved it in front of her nose. She stretched forward and licked it. I had her and I knew it! She turned her head, bawled something at the calf, probably "Let's go!" and slowly lumbered toward me with her tongue leading, reaching for the cube. Stormy trotted along beside her on the other side of the fence.

I slowly walked backward toward the gate with my arm extended, range cube in hand, letting Midnight get a lick now and then. When she started to lose interest, I let her eat the cube and then offered another one.

Walking backward in a pasture so you can't see where you're going almost always guarantees a foot-plant in a cow pie. I knew immediately what happened when I took a step backward and my foot slipped in something mushy. But, other than maintaining my balance, I had a bigger issue to deal with so just kept walking backward.

When we finally reached the gate, I opened it and Midnight shot through to her calf. Not what I wanted. I shook the bucket to get her attention, then dumped the remaining cubes on the ground. She trotted back through the gate and Stormy followed. I shut the gate and life was good!

No walk of shame on this trip back to the house. I did my farm wife happy dance!

* "Don't Fence Me In"—Cole Porter and Robert Fletcher, 1934.

Creek of So Close, Yet so Far

Since that first experience reuniting a separated pair, several followed. Sometimes the barrier was a fence, but on a few occasions, it was a creek. The separation was invariably a point where the bank on either side was steep, and neither cow nor calf could get down one side and up the other without risking injury. Somehow they both knew this.

What they couldn't figure out was there were points nearby where the banks were lower and not as steep. The cow and her calf just stood on their respective sides of the creek and bawled at each other—so close, yet so far. Bill's philosophy was "Leave them alone. They'll figure it out." Well, I just couldn't ignore that bawling. The poor little calf was no doubt hungry and missed its mama. Mama knew it was suppertime and, aside from getting relief from the pressure building in her udder and teats, she knew she had to feed her baby *now*.

This scenario gets me and I cave every time. I already knew attempting to herd a calf was an exercise in futility, so I got behind the cow and gently herded her toward an area where she could safely cross the creek. She lumbered along quite willingly as if she knew where she needed to go. She crossed over, went to her calf and it immediately started sucking. No problem. Maybe this was just a game they liked to play and I was such an easy mark!

Shooting the Gap

A recent reunification effort had a surprising resolution—even Bill couldn't believe it.

There are two ways to get from one side to the other of a barbed wire fence if there isn't a gate handy: either over or through it. The method chosen is determined by one's inseam measurement. Bill is usually able to climb over. Then he puts his foot on one of the lower strands and pushes it down while grabbing the next higher strand and pulling up, creating a gap for me to climb through. When alone, I struggle through, occasionally getting hung up and ripping holes in my clothes. That's why I have designated "farm clothes."

Starting out on a recent evening walk, sans Bill, I heard a calf bawling and a cow's answering bawl. Uh-oh! I knew the situation behind the duet of bawling before I even looked: a separated pair. They were about a hundred yards ahead of me and nowhere near a gate. The cow was fussing while pacing back and forth; the calf was bawling and trotting along the fence, following the cow. I walked along the fence and found one strand of wire hanging low for the length of three fence posts. The staple that fastened the wire to the middle post was missing. The calf had apparently walked through the gap.

I walked beyond the gap to check the ear tag of the cow and identified the pair as #9's. Not good news. Mama #9 had a flighty disposition and was even now heading toward the timber. So all I had left to work with was the calf. Judging from past experience, it was ridiculous to even hope the calf would come back through the gap. But it was the only option I had.

I reviewed the logistics: From where I was standing, the fence gap was behind me. The calf was two fence posts or about ten yards ahead of me. Next I reviewed the options. Walk backwards toward the gap, hoping the calf would follow me, see the gapping fence and walk through. Or, I could circle around behind it and try to drive it through the gap. While I was pondering strategy, the calf slowly walked toward me, reducing the distance between us to one fence section. Then, a third wild, totally improbable option entered my head. No, impossible! Wouldn't work, I argued with myself. Impossible or not, I slowly raised my foot and pushed down on the lowest wire strand, grabbed the next highest strand with my hand and pulled up. The calf shot through the gap and ran to the timber to find its mama. *Unbelievable!*

Bill arrived home a couple of hours later, and I related the amazing feat to him. He couldn't believe it.

Sometimes you just get lucky!

BOOMER SOONER BOVINES

Buying cattle sight unseen from an out-of-state cattle trader has the potential to turn out like buying a pig in a poke, or whatever the bovine equivalent. Digital technology and the internet are valuable tools that keep the transaction from being a completely blind purchase. High resolution pictures are just a couple of clicks away. However, two of Bill's key criteria in buying bred cows can't be conclusively determined with pictures, no matter how many pixels they contain: stage of pregnancy and temperament.

Bill had responded to an ad placed in an agricultural publication by a cattle trader in Oklahoma who was selling bred cows. The delivered price was a couple hundred dollars per head under the sale barn price for similar cows in our area. Bill specified his criteria to the trader: cows four- to six-years-old, bred to have fall calves, and no wild temperament, a/k/a high-headed bitches. The trader assured him he had plenty of cows to fit the criteria and he emailed pictures.

For the most part, Bill liked what he saw in the pictures except for a few cows that displayed prominent Brahma genetics. Bill's opinion of Brahma cattle was they tended to be high-strung, something he didn't want to deal with. He reminded the trader of his selection criteria, then agreed to buy 10 cows, preg-checked and delivered.

Brahma Cattle 101 – Brahma cattle originated in India and are the most common breed of cattle in the world. The breed is sturdy and the animals tolerate harsh conditions well. The most widely-recognized physical characteristics are: large hump over the shoulder and neck; upward-curved horns; long, droopy ears, except when on alert at which time they extend horizontally out from the head; and excess skin that hangs down from the neck and midsection. The navel protrudes out from the loose skin under the mid-section, giving the appearance of an enormous "outtie." Temperament of Brahmas is a debatable issue. Lovers of the breed claim these animals are docile as long as they are handled gently and not bred to an animal of an aggressive breed. Other cattlemen claim the high-headed temperament is inbred in the Brahma breed. And so it goes. Bill's experience puts him on the side of the inbred temperament theorists.

The day before the cows were to arrive, he called the trader to verify the delivery time and get specific details of the cows. The trader had apparently "forgotten" some of Bill's criteria. Most of the cows were on the high side of the age range specified and some were even older; the projected calving time was definitely winter/spring, not fall. Bill's reaction was immediate and succinct, "No deal!" The trader countered with, "I can't sell you what you want at the price you want to pay!" A heated debate ensued. Finally, the trader reluctantly agreed to the original terms.

The trader lived south of Tulsa and would send his brother north with the load. In order to make the round trip in one day, he planned to start loading the cows before dawn; take them to the vet where they would be unloaded, preg-checked, and reloaded; then arrive at our place in the early afternoon.

Preg-Checking 101 - A/K/A Basic Rectal Palpation. As its name implies, this procedure is performed to determine whether or not a cow or heifer is pregnant, and how far advanced the pregnancy is. To perform the procedure, the cow is first confined in a squeeze chute or head gate. (Following a cow around a pasture trying to stick your arm up her rectum is not advised.) The checker puts on a shoulder-length plastic glove, then lubes the hand with the bovine ob/gyn equivalent of *KY Jelly*. The tail is lifted to reveal two holes: the anus, directly below the tailhead, and the vulva, which is below the anus. Or, as they were known at our farm before I knew what stuff came out of which hole, the *high hole* and the *low hole*. In preg-checking, the hand and arm are inserted into the rectum, not the vulva, as doing so could cause an abortion by dislodging the cervical plug. The arm is extended as far as possible into the rectum at a slight downward angle. The reproductive tract of a cow is about three feet long, so the checker's arm will be buried up to the shoulder. The tract is also located below the rectum so the checker's hand should be palm down. If the checker feels a lump through the rectal wall, that is the fetus and the cow is, indeed, bred. In later stages of pregnancy, the checker will feel head, nose, feet and movement when feeling the calf fetus. Once the examination is complete, the arm and hand are withdrawn from the rectum. Oh, one more thing: It's advisable to scoop out any cow poop present in the rectum—there will be poop and very likely a lot of it!—when first inserting the hand and arm. Otherwise, the checker risks dragging out mass quantities of the stuff onto him/herself when withdrawing the hand and arm from the rectum. If the preg-checking procedure sounds just too incredibly gross, trust me when I say it's much faster and easier than waiting for a cow to pee in a plastic cup!

After a couple of phone calls to verify directions and one wrong turn that put him at our neighbor's place a half mile away, the trader's brother rolled in about mid-afternoon. The cows were unloaded into the corral. As soon as they cleared the trailer, four of them tossed up their heads and stampeded to the far end of the small corral pasture. Coincidentally, these four cows exhibited suspiciously predominant Brahma physical characteristics.

However, to put this in the cow's perspective: Someone woke me at 5:00 a.m., which would be his first and, most likely, fatal mistake; loaded me into a stock trailer with nine other females in various stages of pregnancy; hauled me to the vet; unloaded me into a small corral; herded me into an alleyway then prodded me into a chute; closed the front gates around my neck and narrowed the side walls until they squeezed tight around my bulging girth; rammed a latex-gloved hand and arm down my rectum and proceeded to maul my insides, including my unborn baby; prodded me out of the chute and, eventually, back into the stock trailer with my crankier-by-the-minute traveling companions that were subjected to the same treatment; hauled me on a five-hour trip on a warm summer day with no pit stops for water or grass, which sent all 10 of us into cud-withdrawal; then unloaded me into a strange corral. I would have ripped somebody's head off!

Bill and the trader's brother came to the house to complete the transaction. Bill expressed his dissatisfaction with the obvious Brahma genetics of the cows, concerned they would be high-strung. The trader's brother assured him they would gentle down and, besides, they would produce great calves. Bill was skeptical about the "gentle down" part.

In an exchange of mutual distrust, Bill phoned the vet who had preg-checked the cows to verify the information on the written sheet the brother gave him; the brother called Bill's bank to verify sufficient funds were in the account to cover the check. Both phone calls were completed with mutually satisfactory results. Deal sealed.

Bill had already put out hay and water so he left the cows to settle down from their arduous journey. Late in the evening, he went out to the corral to check on them and give them grain. Six were restlessly pacing around the small pasture, mooing in what could only be translated as dissatisfaction with their quarters; however, they did come to the trough for grain. The four cows that had raced to the corner were still there and couldn't be tempted with grain.

The following morning, Bill went back out to the corral, hoping to be able to turn the Okies out into a larger pasture. Something didn't look right, so he did a head count and came up one short. His verbal reaction, *"Gentle temperament, my ass!"* was likely the least of it. Whatever followed could peel paint off the gates and the side of the barn!

He checked ear tag numbers against his delivery sheet. #167 was missing. The gates were all secure and the corral fences were all in good condition, so the only escape route was *over* the fences. He jumped into the mini-truck and roared off to search our 160 acres for the fugitive, hoping one-tenth of his investment wasn't already half way back to Oklahoma.

After several hours of driving pastures and walking heavy timber on our land and adjoining neighbors' land, he returned to the house for lunch, still fuming but also dejected. After lunch, he drove around the neighborhood, hoping to spot that "Brahma bitch." No luck. After another day of intense searching with no results, he was desperate enough to suck up his ego and suffer the extreme embarrassment: go talk to the neighbors, admit he bought a wild cow that was now on the lam, and ask them to notify him if they spotted her. Bill prides himself on the gentle nature of his herd so this was the lowest of low points for him.

Bill kept the remaining nine cows shut up in the corral pen for several days, then released them into the next pasture. They nervously trotted several hundred yards, then abruptly stopped and bunched up. They took off again at a fast trot back and forth across the pasture. Finally, they bunched up near the gate into the north pasture. Bill hopped in the truck, drove to the gate and opened it. They trotted through to their new home for the next six months. If they didn't settle down, they could be permanent residents because he would never get them back to the barn!

Several days went by with no fugitive cow sightings. Bill thought it was odd she had not shown up *somewhere*. We gave up on the expectation she would turn up on our property. I was fairly certain she headed south because she was homesick for that Okie red dirt.

A friend of Bill's invited him to take a long weekend trip to Colorado to help him get his newly purchased vacation home in livable condition. The house hadn't been inhabited for several months and was in need of a deep cleaning—deep, as in *fathoms*. Bill needed a break and, since the cattle were on grass and self-sustaining, I encouraged him to go. Besides, he might just pick up some cleaning skills I could exploit in the future.

The day Bill left for Colorado marked the sixth day since the cow went AWOL. That evening, Cricket and I went for our daily walk. We passed through the gate into the north pasture and saw the cows congregated near the pond: the nine Okies with their blue ear tags, six of our cows with yellow tags and five of last year's heifers that were destined to be next year's first-calf heifers.

We continued on our usual route heading east along the south perimeter of the pasture until we reached the corner post, then turned north, went down a small steep hill, and followed a path beside a barbed wire fence, which divided our timber from a neighbor's property. We were strolling through an area we call the "deer crossing," so named because a major deer thoroughfare intersected with our path at this point, when I heard a crashing noise off to my left. I looked in the direction of the noise, expecting to see one or more deer leap out of the timber and over the fence. Instead, what I saw halfway up a hill was a black hindquarter and tail, heading up the hill as fast as it could crash through the underbrush. Then it disappeared over the top. *Omigosh!* Was that fleeing double rump roast our missing cow?

A foot and hoof chase of a distraught and disoriented cow could only end in disaster in too many ways to count. My only option was to go back to the pond and repeat the head count, focusing on the blue tags. We fast-walked out of the timber and circled around to the pond. I recounted, came up with nine blue tags plus the six other cows and five heifers, for a total of 20. As unlikely as it seemed, the cow in the timber had to be #167. The questions tumbled over each other: Where had she been? Had she left our property, missed her friends and found her way back? Had she been hiding out in our own timber for the last six days? Whatever the answer, she had jumped over at least two fences to get from the corral pen to the north pasture.

The next evening when we headed out on our walk, the cows weren't in the lower section of the pasture near the pond. I assumed we would find them somewhere along the way. One cow might hide out, but not *20*. We followed our usual route and found them congregated in the southeast corner where we turn north. I started working my way through the herd, counting blue and yellow ear tags. Focused on counting, I didn't see how it all started, but suddenly the cows stampeded hell-bent for leather down the hill and through the deer crossing, tearing up chunks of grass and scattering sticks and dirt clods with their thundering hooves. Then they rounded the curve to the west and disappeared from sight. I just stood at the top of the hill and watched, horrified one of them would step in a hole and go down, causing a multi-cow pileup.

In all the years we raised cattle, we'd never had a whole herd full-throttle stampede. I suspected the instigator(s) was one or more of the "blue tag" cows. The only time our gentle cows ran was when hay, grain or range cubes were headed their direction. Even then, they didn't run, just moved at a lumbering trot.

I suddenly remembered Cricket. I lost track of her in the ruckus and hoped she hadn't either joined the stampede or been trampled by it. I found her a short distance behind me near the edge of the timber, sniffing around a fallen dead tree, probably hoping to roust timber critters inhabiting the hollowed out trunk. I called her and we set off to find out if we still had cows in the pasture, or a trail of wrecked fences.

We followed the path out of the timber into a clearing bordered by a creek. Across the creek was a grassy area, then a fence separating the pasture from our cropland. Beyond the cropland was a road. I didn't see any cattle nor did I see a dust cloud drifting over the field or road.

We walked through the clearing that would take us toward the pond. As we neared the pond, I started seeing cattle. Some were grazing, some were in the pond. Everybody seemed to be nonchalantly going about their business as if the stampede had never happened. "Who us? Stampede? You must be mistaken. Those were someone else's cows!" Yeah right, sister!

I restarted my head count, beginning with the blue tags. "1, 2, 3...8, 9, 10." *Ten?* Ten blue tags would mean #167 had joined the herd. I recounted and still came up with ten. Disbelieving, I slowly walked through the herd, getting only close enough to read tag numbers. Most of the blue tags were still skittish and I didn't want to set off another stampede. Two of the cows were hanging back on the fringe of the group. I finessed my way around several cows until there was only one left between me and the two. Then my barrier decided to walk away, leaving about fifteen yards of clear space between us. I expected them to turn and bolt for the timber, but they just stood and warily watched me watch them. One of them lowered her head and pawed the dirt, a warning sign I should not attempt to advance further. Reading the tag numbers at that distance without my glasses would be a challenge, but I needed to get it done and get out of there. I squinted and was able to make out a 166. The other tag was faded so I squinted and leaned forward until I could barely make out the number. It was 167. *Hot dang!* It *was* her. I very slowly moved away from the cows so as not to startle anyone, then headed for the house.

Un-believable! After six days of avoiding anything that remotely resembled or smelled like a human, she just stood there in front of me. Bill would never believe it.

Jared's Colorado vacation home was located in an area of spotty cell coverage but I was able to call and pass along the good news. I didn't talk to Bill. Jared said he was down at a small cabin on the property cleaning the bathroom. "*Cleaning the bathroom?!*" I replied incredulously to that news. "Thanks. That's good to know." Uh-huh!

Proud Mary, one of the Boomer Sooner Bovines and mother of Credence. An atypical example of cows in our herd—the result of buying sight unseen. But, so far, she raises good calves and did "gentle down."

In the next couple of weeks, most of the blue tags settled in to their new life in Kansas except for three with the most predominant Brahma genetics: numbers 166, 167 and 170. Bill wanted to name those cows after legendary bulls from the Professional Bull Riders' rodeos. I wasn't in favor of naming cows after famous bulls so he only named #166 after one of the bulls, "Panhandle Slim," which was shortened to just "Slim." #167, who spent six days hiding out in our timber, was named "Timber Girl"; #170 became "Proud Mary," because, as Bill said, she held her head up as if she was exceptionally proud of herself. Later, when she calved, I named her calf "Credence," after the 1970's pop music group, *Credence Clearwater Revival.* We didn't name any of the other blue tag cows.

When Timber Girl disappeared and particularly after the stampede incident, Bill decided if he ever got the wild cows back up to the barn and in the trailer, they were going to the sale. He didn't want their wild temperament rubbing off on his tame cows. That summer was hot and terribly dry so Bill started feeding hay in August. Proud Mary finally came around, mingled with the other cows and came to the bale feeder to eat. After she had her calf, Bill granted her a reprieve from the sale barn fate since she had tamed down, produced a fine calf and was a good mother. In time, I was even able to get her to eat range cubes out of my hand—quite a turn-around!

But Slim and Timber Girl hung back on the edge of the group for several weeks, not coming forward to eat until Bill left the area. Finally, Timber Girl began to shove her way into the herd around the feeder. Slim still loitered on the edges, ready to bolt if a human even looked her way.

September rolled around and, with it, high school football. On Friday evenings, when Bill was away officiating games, I would take a small plastic bucket of range cubes along when Cricket and I walked, so I could hand-feed the tame cows. All I had to do was rattle the bucket and they came running. I dumped a pile of cubes on the ground and most of the cows rushed in for the treat. While they were gathered around, I fed cubes out of my hand to those who would take them.

At first, both Timber Girl and Slim would hang back when I rattled the bucket. After a few days, Timber Girl worked her way into the crowd gathered around the cubes. But if I tried to offer one to her, she backed away. Okay—now I had a mission: Get Timber Girl to eat range cubes from my hand.

Knowing she didn't like to be approached, my plan required stealth. The next evening when I took the cows their snacks, I picked through the cubes in the bucket until I found the longest one, which was about two inches. I very slowly knelt on the ground in the middle of the group of 1,300-pound cows, (Did I mention there was an element of danger involved?) put my hand on the ground near the pile of cubes and slowly extended my arm until the cube was under her nose. Without looking up, she reeled out her tongue to grab one end of the cube...until she realized my hand was on the other end. She snorted and jerked back. Oooh...so close!

From High Heels to Gumboots

Undaunted, I tried the stealth method of hand feeding a few more times but without success. A few of the yearling heifers had become overly aggressive about eating cubes out of my hand. One nipped my hand and drew blood; another one nearly swallowed my hand. If I didn't feed them, they butted and shoved me. For my own safety, I stopped the hand feeding unless Bill was along to provide a distraction to the aggressive heifers.

By mid-October, 64 out of 70 cows had calved, including all of the Okie blue tags except Timber Girl and Slim. Even though their temperaments had improved since the day they first set hoof on our place, we speculated the skittishness would return once they had calves and the maternal protective instinct kicked in. Bill wasn't optimistic he would be allowed to ear tag either calf. I assumed the mothers would hide in the timber until their calves were half grown.

Timber Girl was starting to "bag up," meaning her udder was expanding. This continued for several days until the udder became so large she was forced to waddle around it with her back legs. Bill made a passing comment about having enough milk for twins. *Was he serious?!* My assessment was she didn't have enough girth through her midsection for twins. Granted, she was big, but *that big?*

One evening in late October, we started out on our walk. Bill drove the mini-truck to the north pasture to haul buckets of grain to the cows. Cricket and I followed on foot and met him at the feed bunks. While he finished feeding, I did a quick check for Timber Girl. She was usually easy to spot in a group where all the cows were black because she had the distinctive Brahma flap of skin under her midsection—the "outtie" navel.

"Timber Girl isn't here," I informed Bill. We jumped in the truck, Cricket hopped into the back and we started driving around the perimeter of the timber, peering intently through the trees trying to catch site of her.

Fortunately, most of the foliage had died in a recent freeze and visibility through the timber was good. As we approached an area that was a popular maternity ward in the past, I spotted her. She was on her feet and facing away from us. Bill pulled the truck up to the edge of the timber, grabbed a pair of binoculars, then slowly and quietly crept through the trees. He focused the binoculars, watched for a few seconds, then moved around to get a side view. He worked his way back to the truck without her ever knowing she was observed.

"I'm pretty sure it's twins," he announced. "I saw what looked like one calf sucking but something wasn't right. So that's when I moved around to get a different angle. I'm sure I saw two calves, each sucking on a tit."

Oh boy! Twins could present another complication if she didn't claim both calves. If she abandoned one of them in the timber, it would likely end up as coyote bait before we could find it.

We didn't expect Timber Girl and her calves to leave the timber for at least a couple of days, if not longer. She could probably sustain herself on grass for a while, but she needed water and would have to leave the timber to go to the creek or pond. After two or three days, it would be critical for her to have nutrients from hay and grain.

The next evening we watched for her when we walked. We found her in a different location in the timber. Bill tried to walk in part way to see the calves, but she saw him and fled. I saw only one calf go with her. I was never really convinced she had twins and Bill was starting to doubt what he thought he saw. He couldn't be absolutely sure until he found two calves.

For the next few days, we saw her every evening either in the timber or out on the edge of it. When she saw us she would trot away and one calf would follow. We never saw a second calf.

The next Friday evening, Bill had a football game and wasn't home to walk with us. While I was focused on spotting Timber Girl and her calf, I lost track of Cricket. As I headed toward the gate I yelled, "Cricket, come!" After several calls, she finally bounded out of the timber with something in her mouth. From a distance, it looked like a bent stick; judging from the proud tilt of her head, I assumed it was something of greater value, at least to her. When she came to me I confiscated her treasure. It was two small bones connected by a joint, like a knee. There were small traces of black meat around the joint, but the bones had been picked clean. The bones had belonged to a very young animal, like a fawn, coyote pup or calf.

When I showed Bill the bones, he said they had to be from the missing twin. He was vindicated. "I knew I saw two calves, side by side, each sucking on a tit!" he exclaimed.

After a week of once again hiding out in the timber, Timber Girl finally rejoined the herd and showed up for hay and grain. She was very protective of her surviving calf and even butted away other calves when they approached to check out their new prospective playmate. Then one morning as he was feeding, Bill saw the grayish-white evidence of scours—diarrhea—

From High Heels to Gumboots

smeared on the calf's butt. It would need an antibiotic injection or it would likely weaken and die of dehydration.

Giving this particular calf a shot would not be an easy task. It was still active, hopping around and acting like a normal calf, so it wasn't yet sick to the point of becoming weak. Then there was Timber Girl to contend with. If Bill caught the calf and it squalled, or if she even saw Bill messing with her calf, she would go ballistic, as would her friends if she summoned reinforcements. This didn't look good!

The next morning, Bill loaded his pistol-grip syringe with antibiotic and headed out to feed. He dumped grain in the feed bunks and the cows, including Timber Girl, crowded around to eat. He found her calf standing with a group of calves. He reached out and gently grabbed one of its hind legs. The calf just stood there, no squalling and no struggling. He inserted the needle into the calf, pulled the trigger releasing the antibiotic, eased the needle back out and walked away. Timber Girl was still chowing down at the feed bunk and never knew what happened. Bill's life as one of the luckiest cattlemen on earth would continue.

Almost two weeks after Timber Girl's calf was born, on an evening when Bill had a football game, Cricket and I were on the last leg of our walk nearing the area where the feed bunks and bale feeder were located. The cows were scattered around near the bunks, across the creek and across a shallow ravine. Bill hadn't mentioned whether or not Slim was showing early signs of impending birth, but knowing she was probably the next one, I took a quick look around the herd. I found Timber Girl but didn't see Slim. Slim also possessed the Brahma "outtie" navel so she was easy to spot.

A more in-depth search would be required. The situation was complicated by the fact that Bill had rotated cattle in and out of that pasture, and the last time he told me how many cows were in it I wasn't paying close attention. Consequently, I didn't know the number. I walked the area around the hay and grain feeders, went across the creek and circled back around to check a couple of ravines for Slim—no sign of her. But I did count 19 cows. Mental Post-It Note: Next time, pay attention.

The sun had set and there wasn't enough light remaining to check the timber so we went back to the house. Bill wouldn't be home until late and there was no point in leaving a note. He couldn't do anything until morning.

The next morning when he went out to feed, he found Slim and her calf in the timber. The calf was up and having breakfast so he left them alone. Unlike Timber Girl, Slim stayed in the timber only two days, then brought her calf out and rejoined the herd. This was a surprise, considering how stand-offish she was prior to calving. Even more surprising, Bill was able to ear tag the calf. Slim was preoccupied eating hay and her calf was lying on the ground on the opposite side of the bale feeder. Bill quietly slipped up to the calf and straddled it to hold it down while he grabbed the ear in one hand and positioned the tagger on the ear. The calf woke up and squalled, bringing Slim around the bale feeder at a dead run. Bill clicked the tag in place and jumped up just as Slim barreled up to her calf. She inspected the tag, licked her calf's ear, then lowered her head and pawed the ground at Bill. He had accomplished what he set out to do so he left.

In November, Bill started the process of moving cattle to the ranch where they would spend the winter. He had already vowed that if he ever got Timber Girl, Slim and their calves near the barn, they were headed to the sale. The cows were good mothers, and their calves looked great and were gaining well. But there was still the temperament issue. Both had improved considerably but Bill didn't trust them. The journey from our north pasture to the stock trailer was only about a quarter mile; from the perspective of getting those two high-strung Brahmas and their calves secured in the trailer, it could turn out to be much longer.

The other cow/calf pairs were already transported to their winter quarters. All that remained were seven heifers, which would be bred before they left, and Slim and Timber Girl and their calves. Bill was giving them grain in a feed bunk every day. He gradually moved the feed bunk closer to the corral area and then into the catch pen, so they would become accustomed to coming in to eat.

The departure date arrived. The truck and trailer were backed up to the loading chute and the trailer rear gate was open in readiness. The cows, their calves and the heifers came into the catch pen area to eat. Bill closed the gate behind them, herded the two calves into the alleyway and shut that gate. He ran them along the alleyway, into the trailer and shut them in the front compartment. So far, so good!

The cows were standing at the alleyway gate watching Bill disappear into the trailer with their calves. When he opened the gate they charged through and ran into the trailer. So did one of the heifers. No problem—he could sort her off at the sale barn and bring her home. Bill shut the trailer gate, jumped in the truck and headed for the sale barn.

Somewhere between our farm and the sale barn, he changed his mind about the heifer and decided to sell her also. Compared to her peers, she was short in length and younger than the others, had not come into a heat cycle, and just wasn't up to his standards.

Bill arrived at the sale barn, drove to the unloading pen area and opened the trailer gate. Those Okies charged out of the trailer, bellowing and tossing their heads, sending the sale barn workers scrambling to the top rungs of the pen panels. The cows and calves ran into an open pen and the gate was slammed shut. The heifer was shut into another pen.

The sale barn manager told Bill they probably would sell the cows as kill cows. Once prospective buyers saw that Wild West show in the sale ring, nobody would want them as additions to a herd. The calves would be sold as bucket calves. The heifer would sell as a feeder heifer, i.e., she would go to a feedlot, be fattened and sold to be butchered.

Bill came home relieved the ordeal was finally over. I wouldn't be convinced it was really over until after Bill verified with the sale barn that they had, indeed, been sold. I was fully expecting a call from law enforcement notifying us the Boomer Sooner wrecking crew had leveled the town. Fortunately, it never came.

June Hilbert

ATYPICAL DAY ON
THE HILBERT FARM

If you've ever looked at an issue of *Farm & Ranch Living* magazine, you've seen the section titled "Farm Family Diaries." These articles are month-long diaries from families in four different states detailing their day-to-day life on the farm. Bill and I experienced a series of events one day that inspired me to start my own "Farm Family Diary."

Friday, August 26:

6:30 am – Bill was awakened by a neighbor returning home from working the night shift at Goodyear. As the neighbor roared by in his near-mufflerless truck, gravel hit the side of our house.

6:45 am – Bill couldn't go back to sleep. When checking calves in one of the rented pastures the previous evening, he discovered a couple of the calves had pinkeye. One calf had already lost sight in one eye and now the disease had spread to the other eye, and to another calf. Bill got up, threw on clothes, gathered up his doctoring supplies and headed to the pasture, a 30-minute drive.

Pinkeye 101 – Common infectious disease affecting the eyes of cattle. It is characterized by redness and inflammation of the eyelid and eyeball. The highly contagious disease is spread by flies. It is treatable with antibiotics but, if left untreated, can cause permanent blindness.

8:00 am – The phone rang and woke me up. *Good grief!* I no longer worked on Fridays and was sleeping in after a busy four days at work. I grumbled to the kitchen to answer the phone. It was Bill's fishing buddy.

Was Bill there? No, he's down at the south pasture treating an outbreak of pinkeye. Yes, I'll have him call when he returns. I grumbled back to bed.

8:10 am – Still awake. May as well get up; I needed to pee, anyway. Took care of the pertinent business, dressed, made coffee and settled in my recliner with the newspaper.

9:00 am – Phone rang again. What is this—a call center? If I wanted to be a phone receptionist I could be at work, getting paid for it. The caller was one of the guys on Bill's high school football officiating crew. They were working a scrimmage at one of the area schools that evening. Yes, I would have Bill call him.

9:05 am – Started load of laundry left from Colorado vacation. I didn't get it all done last weekend when we arrived home. Ate breakfast of yogurt, fresh blueberries and homemade granola. Clipped coupons and balanced checkbook.

9:35 am – Unloaded and reloaded washer. Hung first load on the clothesline.

9:50 am – Bill arrived home and I remembered to give him the messages. Sometimes I forget. My excuse is I don't like to bring work home with me. He returned the call to his fishing buddy, who had a problem and needed advice on his rights under the Kansas Agricultural Lease Law. The problem involved 10 acres of fertile river-bottom land he rented to grow sweet corn, cantaloupe and watermelons to sell at his roadside stand; the tractor and equipment he took to the rented land to tear out what little remained of the melon crop since they were past prime; the landowner, who was scavenging the post-prime melons to sell at *his* roadside stand; and the same landowner, packing heat, who blocked the friend from entering the field to finish tearing out the crop. Said landowner also informed him he would need a court order to retrieve his tractor and equipment.

10:05 am – Unloaded washer and hung laundry on the clothesline.

10:20 am – One of the neighbors stopped by and informed Bill three German Shepherds were chasing cattle in the neighborhood. He spotted them in his pasture, which he leased to the local vet who raised prize longhorn cattle. The dogs crossed to the next pasture and were moving in our direction. The vet had arrived armed with his rifle and was driving the pastures looking for the dogs. The neighbor, armed with his rifle, was headed to help. Bill grabbed his .30-06 and joined the posse. As he jumped into his pickup, I yelled, "Don't shoot each other!"

From High Heels to Gumboots

10:30 am – Watered container flowers outside. We had experienced a prolonged dry spell with temperatures in the triple digits so the flowers looked pretty grim.

10:50 am – Phone rang—again. It was someone with a vet supply company returning Bill's call about ordering more bovine antibiotics. Some of our cattle at home also had pinkeye and we were running low on antibiotics.

11:30 am – Bill returned home. No sign of the marauding dogs. They would live to chase cattle another day. They were also dogs of interest wanted for questioning in connection with the disappearance of another neighbor's chickens. Bill returned the call to the vet supply company.

11:45 am – Bill walked to the mailbox and brought in the mail. There were two envelopes addressed to him from a law firm in Topeka. The letters advised legal action would be taken against the local water district board, of which Bill is a member, by two former employees of the district unless their demand$ were met. The claims were wrongful termination. I perused the mail. Nothing with my name on it. Good! Nobody wanted to sue me.

11:55 am – Took down the laundry, brought it into the house, folded and put it away.

12:10 pm – Whew! What a morning! Made second cup of coffee and sat down at the computer to start compiling the morning's activities for my latest book chapter idea, a farm diary similar to those printed in *Farm & Ranch Living* magazine.

12:20 pm – Phone rang—*again!* The neighbor up the road, whose pasture we rent, called Bill for status of cattle-chasing dogs. She was hopeful of their demise and disappointed to learn it didn't happen. She's also on the water board with Bill, and they discussed the latest development in the saga of the rural Watergate district.

12:45 pm – Bill went outside to clean up tree limbs and debris left in the yard by a recent wind and rain storm. *Ahhh!* Peace and quiet at last. I can't concentrate on writing when there are distractions.

2:00 pm – Bill came in for lunch, then stretched out in the recliner for a nap. Since the computer sets next to the recliner, and I didn't want to disturb him nor have his snoring disturb me, I went to another room and read.

3:30 pm – Bill went out to mow grass. I went back to the computer, checked emails, then worked on the chapter about Timber Girl.

4:45 pm – Bill came in, cleaned up, packed his officiating paraphernalia for the football scrimmage, and left. That evening marked the beginning of

"Friday Nights Without Bill" for Cricket and me until early November. Made note to self to go to the library and check out DVDs for our chick flick nights.

6:20 pm – Cricket and I went for our evening walk and to check cows for impending blessed events. Fall calving season was beginning and we already had six new calves. Bill left instructions for me to check #62 who, according to his calendar, was due any day.

Author's Note: As I don't wear a watch on our evening walks, I abandoned the time table format at this point. Besides, I wasn't expecting the events that unfolded and, subsequently, lost track of time.

We walked out into the pasture and followed the path along the fence. As we topped the first terrace I looked down the other side and saw a cow lying on the ground. She jerked her head toward us, then struggled to her feet and lumbered in the opposite direction. There was a stream of mucus hanging out of her back end. We had startled a cow in labor.

I didn't know which cow it was and didn't want to spook her further by stalking her to get her number, so we backtracked and detoured around the area. She stopped at the top of another terrace and watched us. Good—maybe she would return to her selected labor and delivery site.

I located the rest of the herd scattered around the north part of the pasture. I circulated among them and found #62. So she wasn't the mother-of-the-hour. We continued on our walk, checked cows in an adjoining pasture, then headed for the house.

Almost an hour passed since we came up on the cow in labor and I wanted to go back and check on her, but without spooking her again. I put Cricket in the house, grabbed a pair of binoculars and set off again for the pasture. The cow was near the area where we found her earlier and lying flat on the ground. *Omigosh—I hope she's not dead!*

I stopped at the top of the terrace, about 50 yards above her, and sighted her through the binoculars. Her side heaved up and down, but the motion was rhythmic like breathing, not the jerky motion of contractions. She was facing away from me and the grass around her was so tall I couldn't see her hind quarters from my vantage point.

I debated on whether to stay and monitor from a distance or go back to the house and return later. I didn't know how long she had been in labor, but wasn't concerned about complications yet. Hopefully, Bill would be home before those became an issue.

I decided to hang around for awhile, hoping to experience the happy moment of birth. The cow was still lying on her side with her head on the ground. It wasn't until later, when rehashing the sequence of events, I realized I had never seen her have actual contractions.

Finally, as dusk settled over the pasture and visibility through the binoculars waned, I turned to head for the house, but stopped for one last look. Suddenly, the cow raised her head. I watched and waited. After several minutes, she stood up, turned around, dipped her head toward the ground and started moving it back and forth in a rhythmic fashion. I couldn't see the calf because of the tall grass, but I knew it was getting its first bath. Hallelujah!

I happy-danced back to the house, showered, poured a celebratory glass of wine and waited eagerly for Bill to return.

About a half hour later, I saw his truck lights as he came around the curve in the driveway and met him in the garage with the good news. He backed out of the garage and headed for the pasture.

He returned awhile later, walked into the kitchen and announced, "The calf's dead."

"*What?!*" I asked in disbelief.

"The calf's dead," he repeated. "The cow was lying on the ground beside it and apparently didn't know it was dead. She was one of those two first-calf heifers I bought back in March. The calf was probably dead when it was born."

I was devastated! This happened on my watch. I hadn't considered the amount of time she could have been in labor before I found her; nor did I pick up on the absence of contractions during the half hour I stood on the terrace and watched.

"Don't beat yourself up over it," Bill consoled, "you had no way of knowing how long she was down when you found her the first time. Sometimes, first-calf heifers just quit pushing. We've had that happen before but I was here to pull the calf. It's just one of the risks of calving heifers, especially when I'm not here for the delivery. It was #98 and she slipped off my radar. Anyway, she has a spooky disposition and you wouldn't have been able to drive her to the barn if you had called the vet. It's just part of life in a cow/calf operation."

"So, what happens to her now?" I asked. "I assume an adoption wouldn't work since this was her first calf so she may not even miss it, and wouldn't know what to do with an adoptee."

"Right," he agreed. "Since she has no previous calf experience it would be risky, especially in this hot weather. I'm not going to mess with it. And, I'm not going to breed her because she'd have a late spring/early summer calf, which isn't in synch with my operation. She's a good-looking cow and will fetch a good kill-cow price. We'll just cut our losses and move on. We still have over 60 cows left to calve."

10:30 pm – We went to bed. Life on the farm goes on.

FROM PIECE OF CAKE
TO PIECE OF COW PIE

As soon as Bill said, "I need you to do something for me," I *knew* what was coming. My farmer's wife intuition told me this would be another one of *those* situations: one which Bill said would be easy, one that sounded easy, but one which turned out to be anything but easy.

It was mid-November and time to gather up the cows and calves from our two pastures and the four rented pastures in the neighborhood, bring them home so they could be worked, then loaded up and taken to their winter quarters 30 miles away. Our farm isn't set up to winter a herd the size of ours. We don't put up silage nor do we have the facilities or equipment to store and dispense large quantities of feed and silage.

Working Cattle 101 – *Working cattle* is a catch-all term in Farmerese that includes one or more of the following hands-on procedures performed on cattle: vaccinating or administering other medications; castrating bulls, either surgically or by placing rubber bands around their testicles; dehorning; preg-checking; ear tagging; spraying with fly repellent; branding; and applying Pour-On, a de-worming and de-licing solution poured on the animal, hence its name.

This year's cattle moving project had already started off badly: our one-ton flatbed farm truck that pulled the stock trailer was in the shop for an emergency engine transplant. Bill took it to his mechanic because he thought it wasn't "running right." The mechanic informed him he was only one or two trailer loads of cattle away from blowing the engine. Major nightmare! The procedure was to have been completed so Bill could use the truck, but the mechanic tried three engines before he found one he felt would be reliable. He offered Bill his own heavy-duty pickup to use, and Bill gladly accepted.

The day of this particular adventure, I left work early to do a couple of errands, including the weekly grocery run. I arrived home, schlepped groceries into the house, then changed clothes, looked over the mail, and checked emails. Pretty normal stuff. Bill wasn't home so I assumed he was on the road somewhere with a load of cattle. I grabbed a jacket and started out the door on the evening walk with Cricket when the phone rang. We have an answering machine with audible caller ID so I paused to catch the message, which began "7 8 5 – 2 7 4 – ." It was Bill's cell number. Answer or flee? He might be stranded somewhere impeding rush hour traffic on a highway so I'd better answer. (You know I'm just kidding about the *flee* part, dear. I wouldn't do that to you!) Besides, the hairs on the back of my neck were standing at attention, and I had a premonition this could lead to another chapter in my farm wife memoirs book.

"Don't walk yet. I need you to do something for me," he requested. Yes, definitely book material.

"What?" I responded, somewhat warily, having been in this same spot more times than I could count.

"I need to load out the cows and calves in Bobbie's pasture first thing tomorrow morning, but I can't load from Bobbie's so they need to be moved over to John's pasture. Take the little truck and go over to John's pasture. Drive to his back fence and go through the little gate to Bobbie's pasture and look for the cows and calves. They're probably at the bale feeder by the pond. Rattle a bucket of range cubes to get their attention, and when they start to follow you, drive the truck back through the little gate. Once they're all in John's pasture, shut the gate and you're done. Piece of cake."

I hadn't quite caught all that, except for the part about cake, so I said "Huh?" He repeated the instructions.

"How many?" I asked.

"All of them!" he replied in that exasperated tone of voice he uses when he's overwhelmed with a project but won't admit it, things are not going according to plan, he's running out of time and/or daylight and I'm acting dense.

"No," I replied with admirable self-restraint. "How many cows are over there?"

"Thirteen cows and twelve calves," he responded with equally admirable self-restraint, because this was information I should have known. Then, apparently he opened the window and his self-restraint flew out because he said, "Just wait until I get home. I'm headed across the Oakland Expressway and I'll be there in a few minutes."

By the time Bill pulled into the driveway, I had changed into farm clothes, filled my little bucket with range cubes and was ready to go. Cricket and I jumped in the mini-truck and followed Bill to the barn. He repeated the instructions and added more: put grain in a five-gallon bucket, and put range cubes in another five-gallon bucket. Apparently my little bucket was too small. As the first few cows go through the gate to John's pasture, dump grain on the ground to keep them occupied so they won't go back through the open gate, and then walk back to Bobbie's pasture with the bucket of range cubes to round up any stragglers.

So, off we went on what I suspected would evolve into another farm adventure. We arrived at the first gate to John's corral, which was open, so I drove through, then jumped out and closed it. A short alleyway led to another gate, which was closed, so I walked over and opened it, jumped back in the truck, drove through, got out and closed that gate. Traversing multiple pastures with gates that must be opened and shut works best using the buddy system. It's a labor intensive chore for one person.

At some time in the past, John's pasture was divided into two pastures. Part of the fence was still in place including the opening for the gate, but the gate was long gone. I remembered from an experience about a week earlier that the ground at the gate opening was deeply rutted with tire tracks. The mini-truck didn't have much ground clearance so if I drove in the tracks, I risked getting high-centered. The truck was equipped with four-wheel drive, but it's useless if the wheels don't touch the ground. I would have to finesse my way along the ridge track between the ruts which was a broken, bumpy path overgrown with weeds; even then, I could still get high-centered. I stopped the truck, fastened my seatbelt and Cricket's, and paraphrased the famous Bette Davis line from *All About Eve* (1950), "Hang on, Cricket, it's gonna be a bumpy ride!" Cricket licked my face as if to say, "Go for it, Mom. I've got faith in ya."

I steered the truck into the rutted obstacle course and navigated carefully along the ridge, trying to straddle the ruts. I was almost through it and indulging in a huge exhale of relief when suddenly the front end of the truck pitched down and slammed into a hole. Our seatbelts kept us from crashing into the windshield. Weeds had grown over the hole so I didn't see it. Fortunately it was shallow, so I gave the little truck some gas and it pulled itself out. I hoped the undercarriage was still intact.

We made it through the opening without further incident and continued through the pasture until we arrived at the little gate to Bobbie's pasture, which Bill had left open that morning when he fed cattle. The opening of this gate is extremely narrow but a week earlier I had driven Bill's Ford F-150 pickup through it without ripping off the side mirrors. Getting the mini-truck through unscathed should be a piece of cake, and it was.

Once through the gate, I started looking for cows and calves. There they were, straight ahead about two hundred yards, on a small hilltop. A couple of the cows heard the truck and trotted toward it. I got out, grabbed the bucket of range cubes out of the back and shook it. That got everybody's attention and they stampeded to the truck. This is the Pavlov theory at work: Bill uses the mini-truck to feed so the cows were expecting a meal. Sorry, girls, this is just a snack.

I jumped in the truck, drove back through the gate and stopped a short distance away. The cows crowded around the truck bed and proceeded to wreak havoc. Some of them found the bucket of range cubes, used their heads to butt it over and started eating. Somebody else found a full bucket of apple pulp and dived into it. A couple more butted around three empty buckets looking for food, then found the spilled range cubes mixed with some loose hay and started munching. The scene was total chaos and I had to fight my way through the melee to get to the bucket of grain. Somebody had her head buried in it and I had to grab her ear and pull to get it out. I staggered away from truck and poured the grain on the ground. They swarmed to it.

While they were occupied, I counted and got 13 cows, the target number. As I started to count calves I happened to look over to the pasture where they came from and saw two calves on the other side of the fence. *Mega-sigh!* I walked back through the gate and circled wide around the calves, hoping to drive them to the gate. They started to head in the opposite direction, but I got around them and herded the little rascals toward the gate and through it.

Next up on the agenda: shut the gate. Three simple words that belie the difficulty I faced. This wasn't one of those tubular steel gates on hinges you just swing shut and fasten the chain and clip. No—this was one of those old gates consisting of four strands of barbed wire strung between three small hedge posts. I had to pick up the end post and drag the gate across the opening, pull it tight, position the bottom end of the post in a wire loop near the ground, then pull the post even tighter and muscle the top loop down over the top end of the post. Bill had said if I couldn't get the top loop over the post, there was baling wire hanging on the fence I could loop around the fence post and gate post, which would hold the gate until he could go over and secure it.

I grabbed the top of the gate post with one hand, gritted my teeth and pulled the post toward me, then slipped the wire loop over the end with my other hand. Yeah! This was truly a Wonder Woman moment!

The top and bottom loops were in place but the gap between the gate post and the fence post looked fairly wide. Wide enough for a calf to slip through? I wasn't sure but wasn't taking any chances. I grabbed a piece of the baling wire and looped it around the posts in the middle and twisted the ends together to cut off any avenue of escape to the old pasture. Bill would call this over-kill; I call it preventative measures. We almost never agree on these concepts.

I turned to walk back to the truck and do the head count on the calves, but there were no calves; nor were there any cows. They were all trotting north to the other half of John's pasture. I looked at the ground where I had dumped the grain and saw the reason why. They had slicked up every last granule and licked the ground clean. Nothing left to eat so they may as well check out the new digs. I got into the truck, started it up and followed them.

Going back to the north half of the pasture meant another trip through the rutted tracks. The path was only about ten yards long but it was ten yards of pure driving purgatory. I fastened our seatbelts, gripped the steering wheel and psalmed, "Yea though I drive through the Valley of the Shadow of Deep Ruts, I shall fear no evil high-centeredness." We bounced slowly along the ridges and were almost home free when the truck lurched over a bump, pitched down and stopped. I pushed on the accelerator, but the wheels just spun. So I did what I should have done before I even started through this rutted obstacle course: put the truck in four-wheel drive. Only I grabbed the emergency brake lever and jerked it up instead of the four-wheel drive lever. The levers are side by side between the seats. Then I couldn't get the brake to release. I felt for a button on the end but couldn't find one. I pulled up further on the brake lever, hoping it would release. It didn't. I felt the end of the lever again, looking for a button. Then I realized there was a button but it was recessed into the end of the lever. I had to push in hard with my right index finger while pushing the lever down with my left hand.

I found the four-wheel drive lever, pushed in its button, which wasn't recessed in the end of the lever, and the little truck crawled out of that purgatory pit. If there is a Patron Saint of Farm Wives in Distress, she must be putting in overtime with me!

Having extricated myself from yet another predicament on this "piece of cake" mission that degenerated into a piece of...uh...cow pie, I drove into the pasture and over to the area where the cows had stopped and congregated. They rushed over to the truck and continued their ransacking of the buckets in the back while I tried to count calves. The magic number was twelve, but I counted ten, not once but twice. I surveyed the pasture but didn't see any cows or calves that might have wandered away from the herd. That could only mean I left two in Bobbie's pasture.

This meant a trip back through the Valley of the Shadow of Deep Ruts, only this time I wouldn't be psalming, I would be blaspheming. It also meant

The mini-truck is the workhorse on our farm. It's also Cricket's truck and where it goes, she goes!

undoing my meticulous job of securing the little barbed wire gate. And the odds of herding two calves from one pasture, through a narrow gate and into another pasture were not in my favor. Calves do not herd well, particularly when there is no cow in sight to draw them. However, I knew successful completion of this mission was important to Bill and would save him time and the hassle of having to round up the calves the next morning.

But, beyond that, this mission became yet another defining moment in my life as a farm wife. I couldn't and wouldn't fail. There would be no going home until *all* of the cows and calves were in John's pasture.

Armed with renewed conviction, I smacked, kicked and shoved a path through the cows pillaging the back of the truck, flung open the door and jumped in, fastened our seatbelts, started the motor and roared back to find the calves. When I arrived at the Valley of the Shadow of Deep Ruts, I stopped, engaged the four-wheel drive—not the parking brake—envisioned myself driving a mini-Sherman tank, and we crawled over, up, and down the ridges straddling the ruts. When we reached the other side, I stopped, disengaged the four-wheel drive and headed for the gate between the two properties. There, I spent several minutes undoing all of my earlier work in fastening the barbed wire gate, then flung the gate to the side and drove through.

I stopped the truck and did a visual sweep of the pasture, but didn't see the two calves. The sun had dropped below the horizon so there wasn't much daylight left. Figuring I would have to drive all over the pasture until I found them, I shifted and started forward when they appeared off to my right. They were running along a fence about a hundred yards away that, with any luck, would take them close to the open gate.

I bailed out of the truck and trotted in their direction, staying behind and slightly off to the side, keeping some distance between us. The object was to keep them moving toward the gate without further spooking them. Very likely, they had been goofing around or taking naps somewhere away from the herd and didn't realize everyone was gone until they got hungry and started searching for their mothers. Now they were alone and frantic.

The calves streaked along the fence until they came to the corner, rounded it and headed for the gate. I sprinted to intercept, hoping to herd them through the opening. They cut around me then veered off to the far side of the pasture. Okay—so we were going to do this hard way, whatever that was, and assumed I was about to find out.

The calves dashed out of sight. I jogged back to the truck. They seemed to be following the fence perimeter so I watched and waited, hoping they would come back around. I was focused on the fence line and almost missed them when they ran up a nearby pond dam and stopped. They had changed course and headed across the middle of the pasture to the pond.

June Hilbert

The calves stood on the pond dam and bawled for their mothers, then took off again. Only this time, they ran in the general direction of the gate. I jumped out of the truck and took off behind them, hoping they would continue on course. They veered off again, cutting across several yards ahead of me. I looked up and saw a large black shape standing on top of a small rise. It was one of the cows searching for her calf. When the calves reached her, she turned and headed for the gate with the calves trotting along beside her. I gasped a breathless thank you to my Patron Saint, turned and walked back to the truck.

I reached the truck, got in and started the motor. By now, it was almost completely dark and I needed headlights. There was no dome light and I couldn't remember which of the two steering column levers turned on the lights. But after a squirt of washer fluid hit the windshield, I knew which one *didn't*.

Once again I had to deal with the barbed wire gate: drag the gate across the opening, stick the gate post into the bottom wire loop, pull the post until I could get the top loop in place, then run the baling wire around the center of both the fence post and gate post, and twist the ends together. Next stop: The Valley of the Shadow of Deep Ruts.

I was too exhausted to psalm or blaspheme so I just stopped, engaged the four-wheel drive, not the emergency brake, and bounced to the other side. There I stopped, disengaged the four-wheel drive and headed for the corral. Before I could even shift into second gear, I was surrounded by a 13-cow welcoming committee, intent on resuming their truck bed ransacking. I slowly plowed through the black bovines in motion, nudging beef out of the way until I reached the corral.

Now I was faced with a challenge potentially bigger than the ruts and the barbed wire gate combined: drive the truck through the first gate into the alleyway, jump out and close the gate before the cows could get through. While I sat there, slumped over the steering wheel, trying to figure out how I was going to pull this off, the Patron Saint of Farm Wives in Distress cleared her throat.

"Ahem! I'll give you one hint how to get out of this one and the rest is up to you. Here it is: I think there are still some range cubes left in that bucket in the back of the truck."

A chorus of hallelujahs, hosannas and all but one or two of the psalms went off in my head. Of course! Grab the bucket, rattle it, walk several yards away from the truck, dump what was left of the cubes on the ground, scramble out of the way so I didn't get trampled, sprint to the gate, open it just wide enough to get the truck through, sprint back to the truck, jump in, race through the gate, jump out, and shut the gate. Piece of cake!

I got in the truck and set my escape plan in motion. It went off without a hitch. I shut and secured the gate just as the cows finished slicking up the range cubes and wandered over in search of more food, reeling out their tongues to lick my hands as I fastened the chain clip. I walked back to the truck, stopped, leaned against the bed, and took a few moments to catch my breath and mouth a heartfelt psalm of appreciation to my Patron Saint of Farm Wives in Distress.

I got back in the truck, drove through the last gate, jumped out and swung it shut, fastened the chain clip, got back in the truck and we headed home. When we arrived, I walked into the kitchen and checked the microwave clock. The green digital display glowed 6:30. We had been gone over two hours.

Another piece of cake farm errand had turned into a piece of cow pie ordeal.

Epilogue—The following Monday at work, the first floor receptionist called and told me there were flowers at her desk for me. I went down and found a beautiful fall bouquet of cut flowers with this note (sic): "Tks for rescuing me from Bobbie's pasture. Calf #700"

Another item for my farm adventure memento collection.

June Hilbert

NON-BOVINE ADVENTURES

Not all of my farm adventures involved cattle. A snake triggered one memorable event.

Snake Slayer

My absolute terror of snakes goes back to when I was 10 years old. It happened during the summer when I spent a week at my grandparents' farm. Granddad had trimmed shrubs around the house and left the brush in the yard overnight. The next morning, he loaded the brush piles into the back of his pickup using a pitchfork. I helped by picking up the small piles using just my bare hands. I picked up one pile, walked over to the truck, stepped up on the running board and threw it into the truck bed. I turned around and started to step down off the running board. Then I saw the snake, lying curled up where I had just picked up brush. I shouted, "Granddad! There's a snake behind you!"

He whirled around and exclaimed, "It's a rattler!"

He attacked it with his pitchfork and finally killed it. I never remembered running from the truck to the porch, but when coherent thought returned, I was wrapped in Grandma's arms and Granddad was carrying off the dead rattler. Once recovered from the immediate terror, I realized this story had great show-and-tell potential. But it was summer and there was no school. I had to be content with regaling my family and friends with my terrifying tale, and with each retelling of the event, managed to lock in a potentially lifelong fear of snakes.

In the early years of our dating and marriage, Bill took a 10-day fishing trip to Canada with friends every year after Memorial Day. My up-close-and-personal encounter with a snake happened during my first year living on the farm at Valley Falls while he was in Canada.

I arrived home from work, changed into running gear and went for a run. I was running competitively at this time and in training. After returning to the house, I went out to the asparagus patch to harvest the day's cutting. I was headed back to the house with a big handful of stalks when I happened to look down and saw a snake curled up in front of my right foot. Without breaking stride, without any conscious thought whatsoever, my body launched itself off my right foot and went airborne into a leap that would have made a broad jumper drool.

Once I hit the ground, standing up by some miracle, I looked back. The snake was still there and didn't appear to have moved. I cautiously edged about an inch closer, trying to get a look at the head or tail to determine whether or not it was a rattlesnake. The head wasn't visible, but I could see the tail and it wasn't adorned with rattles. Whew! But...there were other venomous snakes indigenous to this area, like copperheads. *OK, now what?* It could be a copperhead, or it could be non-venomous, such as a bull snake. Knowing any kind of snake was slithering freely around the yard, I wouldn't set foot out of the house until Bill returned. Also, I didn't want Ginger, our Golden Retriever, to find it in case it was poisonous. The choice was obvious: the reptilian intruder was headed for snake heaven.

Next dilemma: call a neighbor or carry out the execution myself. I despised the thought of being the helpless "green horn City Girl damsel in distress." So I girded myself to be the executioner.

I dashed into the house, taking Ginger with me. I couldn't waste time changing clothes but needed leg protection since I was wearing running shorts. I looked around the back porch for Bill's tall gumboots, couldn't find them and had to settle for a pair of his old army combat boots, vintage 1968 and enormous on me. The leg protection extended just beyond mid-calf and would have to suffice. I didn't take time to lace them up, just clomped out of the house. Next I needed a weapon, preferably one with a very long handle. A quick search of the tool shed yielded a hoe with a handle about five feet long, made of half-inch diameter galvanized pipe. I would have preferred a handle about twice as long, but probably couldn't have lifted 10 feet of galvanized pipe, let alone executed a snake with it.

Protected, armed and dangerous, I clomped across the yard, repeating *I can do this* over and over to myself, until I reached the asparagus patch. Leading with the execution hoe, I stealthily crept up to the snake. The preferred method of killing snakes is decapitation but since the head wasn't visible, I would aim for the middle of the clump of snake and hope the first whack was the death blow. Raising the hoe, I brought it down with all the force I could muster. *Whack!* I looked down expecting to see bloodied pieces of dead snake. Instead, the snake clump came to life as a hissing, writhing beast, striking at the hoe blade and anything else within its reach. Definitely *not* dead! Lifting the hoe to take a second whack wasn't an option unless I wanted to risk getting bitten. Suddenly those combat boots didn't cover nearly enough of my bare legs.

Huge, pounding heartbeats surged up my throat with a seismic force that rattled my teeth and blocked incoming air from reaching my lungs. Yet I stood there on the verge of passing out, with a snake full of murderous rage pinned to the ground, and reviewed my options: Drop the handle and beat combat-boot-clad feet out of there, hoping I didn't trip and fall; or, try working the hoe back and forth and side to side, hoping to eventually saw the snake into pieces. My hands and arms were trembling so violently from the seismic heartbeats that the sawing motion had already started. I applied some murderous rage of my own, increasing the sawing intensity to compensate for the dull-bladed hoe. After a couple of minutes, the hissing and writhing was losing momentum. Finally, snake guts started to ooze out so I lifted the hoe and brought it down again...and again and again and again. All snake movement finally ceased. The beast was either dead or would be soon. And, it was still in one piece. Official cause of death: blunt force trauma.

The next dilemma: disposal of the snake corpse. The only acceptable option was immediate removal from the premises. Not that I *really* thought it would come back to life and hunt me down. No, I would just sleep better knowing it wasn't anywhere on the property. I looked down the driveway to the highway, a distance of about 150 yards—probably far enough. As I picked up the snake with the hoe, I realized transporting a whole lumpy snake was going to be much easier than trying to gather up a multitude of snake pieces. Pieces would have required a container for transport because I refused to carry chopped snake in my hands, gloves or no gloves.

The funeral procession of one slowly clomped down the driveway, carrying the snake to its final resting place irreverently draped over the execution hoe, which was getting heavier by the minute. I finally reached the highway, clomped across and partway down the ditch on the other side. I swung the hoe back then forward to sling the snake as far as possible. Satisfied, I slowly clomped back up the driveway.

The adrenalin tsunami began to subside, and with it came a profound revelation: I had overcome my fear of snakes and did what, in my mind, had to be done. Granted, this one turned out to be a relatively harmless bull snake, although they do have teeth, and not a venomous copperhead. A thought ran through my mind: *What would Bill have done?* The answer: he would have put on a pair of heavy gloves, picked up the live snake and relocated it to the neighbor's pasture. Well, he wasn't here and it was my judgment call. At least I'd sleep tonight.

Another revelation came with the return of my vital signs to normal range, this one painful: All that clomping down and then back up the driveway in Bill's combat boots rubbed off skin and left raw areas on my feet and ankles. I considered this discomfort a small price to pay for such a courageous deed.

When Bill returned home, he went out to the shed to look at the hoe after I complained about the dull blade. "Look what you did to my hoe!" he exclaimed. The galvanized pipe handle that had formerly been very straight now had a definite curve in it—evidence of my vicious attack on that snake.

We still have the execution hoe. It leans against the wall in the tool shed and serves as a testament to my rite of passage when I shed my terror of snakes.

Gumbo Chicken
A/K/A Attack Rooster

As mentioned in my introduction, grandkids were not allowed much hands-on experience with animals on my grandparent's farm. But Grandma let us help her gather the eggs. In those days, my grandparents had a lot of chickens and those chickens laid a lot of eggs. After gathering, the eggs were cleaned, then boxed up in egg crates to sell to Seymour's in Topeka. Those trips to the city with Granddad and Grandma were a real treat!

When I said grandkids weren't allowed hands-on experience with farm animals, I meant *live* animals. We got plenty of hands-on experience with dead chickens. Every summer my mom and aunt loaded up us kids to go to the farm for the annual chicken-dressing event. Our job was plucking feathers off the dead chickens. I've never really understood why this event was called *dressing* chickens. Seems to me we were *un*dressing them by plucking off their feathers.

From High Heels to Gumboots

The most exciting part of the day was watching Grandma whack the heads off squawking, hysterical chickens. The woman could wield a hatchet! Watching a headless body flop around on the ground, spraying blood all over everything, was just morbidly cool. The farm dogs went nuts, barking and racing around trying to pounce on the bodies. The dogs eventually had to settle for chewing up the chicken heads.

Anyway, by the end of the day, we'd take home enough dead, plucked and gutted carcasses to keep us in fried and baked chicken for a year.

When I met Bill, he had a few chickens and a clock-challenged rooster. It never crowed at dawn like a normal rooster. That rooster crowed when a vehicle drove into the yard. It crowed at anything that moved. It even crowed for no apparent reason. But at least it was harmless, unlike the attack rooster I encountered years later.

We'd moved to the 40-acre farm and lived there several years when our neighbors took a trip to Colorado. They asked Bill to look after their place, which they had done for us a few times, and to take care of their chickens: gather eggs and top off the feed and water. No problem, except Bill had a work commitment in the central part of the state and would be gone for a couple of days and nights. The chicken chores were passed over to the logical alternate—me. The first evening, dressed in cut-offs, a tank top and tennis shoes I headed up to the neighbors' place. Why am I always inappropriately dressed for this stuff?

There was a chicken house within a fenced area called the "coop." I grabbed the egg bucket and entered the coop. The chickens were milling around and softly clucking, as chickens do. I think of this as chicken mumbling. I had to wade through the cluck-fest to get to the door into the chicken house. Suddenly, a sharp pain knifed through my thigh. Looking down, I saw a bloody three-inch gash on the side of my thigh just above the knee. *What the...!* I looked around but couldn't see where I had run into anything. I looked at the chickens, still milling around, clucking to each other and themselves. Nobody looked the least bit guilty, but something had put an ugly gash in my thigh.

I continued wading to the door but had only progressed a few feet when something hit me again. Another gash, but this one was not as severe. I heard a flapping noise and looked up in time to see a flurry of white feathers homing in on my bare legs. I raced into the chicken house, slammed the door behind me, gathered the eggs, checked the feed and water—both okay— and prepared to run the gauntlet to the gate as fast as I could wade through the cluster-cluck. This time when it nailed me I saw it: a rooster with two-inch claws sticking out of the backs of both legs. These weapons of mass destruction are known as "spurs." How appropriate!

I escaped the chicken coop with my life and assessed the damage: two gashes and one scratch, all bleeding. I took the eggs into the mud room of the neighbors' house and headed home to dress my wounds. The gashes weren't serious enough to warrant a trip to the emergency room so I thoroughly disinfected the wounds using alcohol (#%$@*!) and applied bandages. The next evening, I wore appropriate chicken coop attire: jeans, long-sleeved shirt and boots!

When the neighbors returned from Colorado, Bill told them about my experience with the attack rooster.

"Oh, well, we forgot to warn you."

Oh yeah, minor oversight! There was a shovel leaning against the chicken house next to the gate into the coop. They used it as a shield and, if necessary, a weapon when they went in.

A few weeks later, the neighbor told Bill they sold the chickens and attack rooster to another neighbor. She is from Louisiana and skilled at Cajun cuisine. The rooster nailed her once and ended up in her cast iron Dutch oven as Chicken Gumbo.

I thought a good posthumous name for that attack rooster was "Gumbo."

A WALK ON THE WILD SIDE

Every evening walk is a potential adventure, especially if Bill is gone. Though the adventures may not be full-scale sagas of epic proportion, suitable for mini-series productions on the RFD Channel, they may be mini-adventures. Even after 25-plus years on the farm, they all still rate as adventures to me.

Dances With Snakes

Even though I earned my stripes as Snake Slayer, a chance encounter with a snake can still startle the holy heck out of me.

As we were returning from our walk one evening, Bill detoured to one of the barns and Cricket followed him. I passed through the last gate and, not being in any particular hurry, meandered along the path toward the house enjoying the early fall evening. I felt something on top of my right foot and, thinking it was a stick and not bothering to look down, lazily shook my foot to dislodge it. As I took another step, I could still feel an object on my foot, so shook it again. This time, something hit my left leg but something was still clinging to my right foot. The *something* now had my attention so I looked down. *Omigosh! A black snake!*

A flash flood of adrenalin gushed through me and I launched into a frenzy of kicking like a Riverdance performer on caffeine overload, trying to fling the snake off my foot. It landed on its back on the ground, and I leaped over it. Probably not smart but it was a reflex reaction. I ran a few steps, then stopped, turned around and looked back. The snake was gone.

The sensation of feeling something on top of my right foot striking at my left leg stayed with me until bedtime. I drifted into sleep wondering what species of snake might slither into my dreams and if some nightmarish Irish jig might be my last dance.

Morning brought profound relief—no snakes on my dream dance card.

Coyotes in the Fog

Unlike the old adage of children being "seen, not heard," coyotes are generally "heard, not seen." They're usually heard after dark, either as a singular howl of communication, or as the cacophony of a pack where all members feel the need to express themselves. I have seen a few coyotes in daylight, often running across the road in front of my car when I'm driving to work in the morning. I've also seen those who unsuccessfully attempted to run across the road in front of a vehicle and ended life on earth as roadkill.

One foggy fall morning, I dragged myself out of bed at the butt-crack of dawn to take the dog for her morning walk and to check cattle. Do I need to actually say Bill was out on a work assignment or have you picked up on this situation by now? Brandy ran out ahead of me into the pasture and was soon swallowed up in the fog. I counted big and little black shapes in the front pasture, arrived at the correct number of both, then headed to the back pasture to hurry Brandy along in her search for just the right spot to conduct her morning business. As I started through the gate I heard Brandy's territorial bark, followed by multiple high-pitched barks. I knew the source of those barks—coyotes. Brandy had apparently rousted out a den.

Frantically I screamed for her to "Come!" but knew it was futile. Even if she could hear me above the noise, she had an unusually aggressive nature for a Golden and wouldn't back down. I feared the worst: my beloved pet would be outnumbered and ripped apart by the savage pack.

The thick fog turned the pasture into an echoless, acoustical vacuum, containing the sound of the frantic barking and giving it the clipped, staccato quality of an automatic pistol. As I started to sprint up a small hill in the direction of the melee, the high-pitched barking suddenly became louder and I couldn't hear Brandy's bark at all. *Oh no!* They killed her and were coming for me! Torn between racing headlong into the white abyss to find my dog and retreating from the vicious pack, I stood frozen. Two shapes streaked out of the fog at the top of the hill, headed right for me—the "pack" of coyotes. Then a third shape crested the hill—Brandy! She had the coyotes on the run. They spotted me and veered off. Brandy gave chase for a few more seconds, then stopped and trotted back to me, looking wonderfully proud of herself.

My heroine!

In the Timber Primeval

Various hazards can befall someone who indulges in poetic musings while walking through timber. Some are relatively harmless but disgustingly gross, like stepping in a cow pie. Tripping hazards, such as rocks, logs, a baby calf napping in tall grass and frozen cow pies can cause injury. I can attest to the fact frozen cow pies are dangerous tripping hazards because it happened to Bill. Still others have the potential to trigger cardiac arrest. I experienced such an event during another wildlife encounter.

Another evening walk, just Cricket and I. She trotted along, happily grinning, thrilled to be partaking of a smorgasbord of sniffing delights. I ambled along while thoughts meandered aimlessly in my head. We left the pasture and followed a path through the timber. I began toying with the phrase "In the forest primeval...," hoping for a Longfellow-esque revelation. Now, my poetic prowess doesn't extend much beyond "Roses are red." But the first time I walked along this path bordered by dense timber, the phrase "forest primeval" flowed out of some forgotten literary memory into my mental musing. Later research revealed this phrase to be from the opening line of Henry Wadsworth Longfellow's epic poem *Evangeline*.* It takes a fairly robust imagination to transcend oneself from timber in Kansas with barbed wire fences and cow pies to an idyllic primeval forest in Nova Scotia lush with "murmuring pines and the hemlocks, bearded with moss, and in garments green."

Our walking and driving path through the "Timber Primeval."

So, I was ambling along the path, communing with Henry Wadsworth, when a horrendous crashing noise jerked me back from Nova Scotia and into near-cardiac arrest. *Yikes!* My primeval timber was tumbling down on me, or so it seemed. I looked up in time to see several wild turkeys fly out of trees directly overhead. The cacophony also got Cricket's attention and she started after them until I called her back. Apparently, the turkeys were settled for the night and we disturbed their tree slumber. I had seen turkeys in our timber on previous walks, but they were on the ground, not in trees; they ran, not flew, for cover when we approached. I was unaware of the thunderous flapping racket their wings make on take-off.

The 10 seconds of excitement for Cricket and cardiac arrest for me were over so we continued our walk.

I bet Evangeline never got the crap scared out of her by a flock of wild turkeys!

*Evangeline by Henry Wadsworth Longfellow, 1847. The poem is set in Nova Scotia.

Alien Cattle Rustlers

An evening walk that starts out with an afternoon phone call from Bill to me at work is a potential adventure. This was the scenario several years ago while we still lived on the 40-acre farm.

Cow #15 delivered her calf late one evening, then they both seemingly vanished from the face of the earth. We both saw them when we were walking but since it was almost dark, Bill decided to wait until morning to tag the calf. When he went out to find them the next morning, they weren't in the location where the calf was born. Bill tramped all over the 40 acres—no cow, no calf. He walked the perimeter to check for holes in the fence or a telltale piece of black hair stuck to a barb in the fence, a sign the cow might have jumped over. Nothing. He walked along the banks of the drainage creek that ran through our property. Again, nothing. He drove around a couple of neighboring pastures. Still nothing.

Bill wouldn't be home until late that evening so he called me at work and advised me to be on the lookout for the pair when I walked. Much as Bill had earlier in the day, I tramped the 40 acres. Fortunately, we didn't have areas of dense timber as we do now, just a few acres sparsely populated with a few trees and nothing that would provide a hiding place for a new mother and her calf. But I searched it anyway.

Finally, there was nowhere else to look. We both covered the pasture, timber and creek. The fence was intact. What was left? Cattle rustlers? It was highly unlikely they would steal only one pair. Alien abduction? Was some extraterrestrial rustler beaming up our cattle, one pair at a time? I've never really been into science fiction, and I couldn't get my head around this one.

The sun was edging below the horizon; daylight was giving way to evening. Defeated, I turned to head back to the house. But something drew my eyes toward the creek, a niggling thought. I had walked the bank along one side only, thinking that was sufficient since the creek was narrow. That thought pulled me back to the creek to walk the length on the other side. The distance was only about a quarter of a mile, so this wouldn't take long.

I started walking at our east property line and followed the winding, mostly dry creek, keeping as close to the edge as I dared. Even though there wasn't much water, I could get hurt if I fell down the bank through brush and fallen trees. As I neared the pond dam toward the west property line, the creek narrowed and the bank on both sides became steeper. Not much likelihood the cow and calf would be in such a narrow, confined area. Anyway, it was getting dark and, even if there were places left to search, trying to find a black cow at night was an exercise in futility. Maybe that alien cattle rustling theory had merit after all!

The only place to cross the creek was below the pond dam so I continued west along the bank, pondering about the size of a flying saucer and the laser intensity necessary to beam up a 1200-pound cow and her 70-pound calf. I just happened to glance over the bank and saw a big black shape. I stopped and inched closer to the edge. The black shape had a head and it turned to look at me, then mooed softly. #15! The calf was lying at her feet against the side of the creek bank. Both appeared to be okay and the cow had just a few inches clearance between her flanks and the bank, so she wasn't trapped. Yeah! Life was good! Cattle-rustling aliens...who believes that stuff anyway?

Bill arrived home shortly after I returned to the house. He drove out to the creek, found the pair and herded them toward the pond dam where they walked up the bank and returned to the pasture.

The next day while I was at lunch, Bill dropped off a bouquet of flowers at my desk. The message on the card was, "June, Tks (sic) for finding me. #15." I still have that card.

June Hilbert

FARM FRESH FILOSOPHIES

I consider myself to be a fairly philosophical sort. My observations during this transformation from City Girl to Farm Wife provided fertile ground to cultivate my "Farm Fresh Filosophies." Some filosophies may yield legitimate insights; others are probably just fertilizer.

HAY FEVER—NOT JUST AN ALLERGY

Hay fever is not just an allergy, although the allergy is prevalent in the country. What I'm referring to is an obsessive-compulsive disorder (OCD) that afflicts farmers during hay season. "Make hay while the sun shines" isn't just a quaint, old saying; it's a mandate. In order to serve healthy, nutritious hay your animals won't turn up their noses at, that won't mold or burn down your barn, the recipe calls for a heaping helping of sunshine accompanied by a gentle to moderate wind. Another way to think of it is: hay has to be blown-dry and styled before it can be baled and stored.

Hay Pyrotechnics 101: Hay that hasn't been properly dried and cured prior to baling has the potential to self-ignite. How it happens: Moisture trapped within bales or stacks of hay creates mold and bacterial growth, and promotes live plant respiration. These processes combine to generate chemical reactions that produce heat and cause a "sweating" action. The sweating drives the moisture throughout the stored bales until it reaches an area of drier hay. This area where wet and dry hay meet has the heat, dampness and insulation necessary for spontaneous combustion to occur.

Apparently, hay fever OCD is contagious and my immune system was vulnerable. This became apparent when: 1.) I found myself checking the online radar weather map eight or ten times a day at my office during hay season; and, 2.) I stood in the sports drink aisle of the grocery store for ten minutes, debating which flavor sports drink to buy for the hay crew. Common sense told me to stay away from anything *pink*! Our hay crew was made up of high school football players so anything that resembled a sissy drink was eliminated. Any blue or clear variety would probably be fine as long as the flavor name was something like "Mountain Blast" or "Cool Ice." So I chose the "Mountain Blast."

Besides buying sports drinks, bottled water and groceries to feed the hay crew after the day's work was done, I also have been drafted into service as a truck driver. I drive the truck pulling a hay trailer while the hay crew picks up bales and stacks them on the trailer. The truck is a one-ton Dodge flatbed and the trailer is called a 24-foot gooseneck hitch, according to my technical consultant, a/k/a Bill.

Simply put, I drove a huge truck pulling an extremely long trailer.

I drove very slowly in the lowest gear while two guys picked up bales off the ground, tossed them up onto the trailer, where another guy stacked the bales in a certain configuration so the bales would not tumble off. Sounds simple. Oh, and I sat on the edge of the seat because the seat adjustment mechanism was broken and the seat position was set for someone about six feet tall. I'm five feet and six inches. Now for the tricky part: The hay meadows were slightly hilly so the ground was terraced to prevent erosion. The trick was to drive over the terraces at an angle, not straight up one side and down the other. The latter method guaranteed becoming high-centered, leaving the truck straddled across the top of the terrace, wheels off the ground, teeter-tottering back and forth. Meanwhile, the driver's stomach has plummeted to the floorboard, due to motion sickness compounded by abject terror. The rescue operation would entail being towed off the terrace by a much larger vehicle, risking damage to both truck and trailer. High-centering also guaranteed getting yelled at by the Hay Operations Manager, a/k/a Bill. On the other hand, driving over terraces at too sharp an angle could cause spillage of the trailer contents: hay and crew.

I'm proud to say I only high-centered once, and it was the trailer not the truck, so I was able to get off the terrace by alternately rolling forward and backward, thereby rocking myself off the terrace. No teeter-tottering, no towing and no yelling!

On one occasion in recent years, a rogue storm blew up out in the central part of the state around mid-day and roared eastward. Bill had over 200 bales on the ground and was still baling. The hay crew kids were scheduled to arrive around 5:00. At about 3:00, Bill looked to the west and saw dark, ominous clouds looming on the horizon. He called my office number on his cell phone from the hay meadow, intending to ask me to pull up the online weather radar map and report the tracking of the storm. Did I mention one of the preferred qualities of a good farm wife is a basic understanding of Meteorology 101? I'd already checked the radar and saw the menacing yellow-orange-red mass threatening the Salina area. When my phone rang and his cell number popped up on my caller ID, I picked up the receiver and warned, "You'd better round up the kids and haul ass!"

I offered to leave work early and come home to drive but Bill recruited Jim, a neighbor, to drive and supervise the loading operation to keep things moving quickly. While Bill continued to bale, Jim and three of the kids started loading the trailer. By the time they arrived at the barn to stack the first load, I was just pulling into the driveway and a couple more kids roared in behind me, jumped out of their cars and raced for the barn. Seconds later they raced back out, hitched our small two-wheeled utility trailer to Bill's pickup, and took off out of the driveway. I threw together ice and drinks in a cooler for the rest of the crew to grab on the return trip to the hay meadow.

With nothing left to do but wait, I paced around the house, frequently checking the online radar map and sipping a glass of wine to calm my nerves. I felt useless and left out of the action. The storm was advancing across Shawnee County and would be on us in minutes. If my car trunk could hold more than a couple of bales, I would have charged over to the hay meadow. Instead, I paced, clicked the Refresh icon to update the radar and sipped wine. Pace...refresh...sip. Pace...refresh...sip. As the first rain drops pelted down, I stepped out of the garage, looked north for the hundredth time...and heaved one *huge* sigh of relief. Then tossed back the rest of my wine.

The guys were headed home in a creeping procession of vehicles loaded with hay bales. In the lead was Jim, driving the one-ton truck pulling the trailer. He was followed by one of the kids driving the pickup pulling the utility trailer, which was so overloaded I could almost hear it groan in protest as it crept up the road. Next in line were two of the kids in their own pickups, bales stuffed into the beds and hanging out precariously over the sides. Bringing up the rear was Bill on his John Deere tractor, pulling the baler.

As the vehicles came down the driveway, they headed off in different directions: The big trailer was backed into one barn, to be unloaded later.

The utility trailer was backed into the machine shed, also to be unloaded later. The kids in their own trucks headed for another barn to unload immediately.

A short time later, the crew plodded wearily to the house through a downpour of rain. They dropped into lawn chairs set up in the garage and dived into bowls of tortilla chips and salsa. I passed around more water and "Mountain Blast." Bill trudged in, collapsed into a chair and I brought him a frosty mug of beer. I also refilled my wineglass. Once everyone had relaxed for awhile, Bill fired up the grill.

The kids earned bonus pay for their dedication to bringing home dry hay. He would have been happy to get *most* of it home dry, but the kids worked their butts off to get it *all* home dry. What a great group of kids!

* * *

Our wedding anniversary is July 12th. If it rains, we get to celebrate. If not, we're putting up hay. (Remember: "Make hay while the sun shines.") I fondly remember our 20th anniversary: After the hay was baled and stacked in the barn, we shared an anniversary dinner of grilled brats, tortilla chips and salsa with the hay crew. When Bill told the guys it was our anniversary, they scolded him for not taking me out for a nice wine and candlelight dinner. Bill saluted me with his frosty mug of beer, saying "Thanks, dear, for your understanding and your help!"

For our 24th anniversary, we were in a non-typical rainy season and had rain the previous night so no haying on that July 12th. We spent our anniversary with a couple who are also farmers. Bill grilled steaks and we had our own fresh corn on the cob, fresh tomatoes and homemade chocolate-chocolate chip ice cream—one of our favorite dinners.

For me, the best thing about hay season is I pick up mega "good wife points!" Would I trade all this for being wined and dined on our anniversary? Not a chance! I'll take being beered and cheered any day!

The Hay Baling Process

First, the swather cuts the grass and swaths it into rows.

Second, raking turns the rows of hay over so the bottom will dry and also fluffs them up so they feed into the baler. This is the Ford 8N tractor I helped pull start in "It's a Man Thing."

Third, baler picks up the cut hay, forms the bale, ties it with wire and pushes it out the back. We still put up little square bales like these, but we now also do the big round bales.

Loading and stacking by hard-working young guys like these enable us to continue putting up square bales.

MARS AND VENUS ON THE FARM

In his book, *Men Are From Mars, Women Are From Venus,* Dr. John Gray proffered the theory that men and women are so totally different beings, it's as if they originated from different planets. Then he provided a unique way for couples to accept and appreciate those differences which, in turn, allows for greater understanding and communication in relationships. A series of books followed, each of which focused on the various types and stages of relationships.

Unfortunately, Dr. Gray failed to provide guidance to a very select group of couples whose individual members are inherently and drastically different: the farm-raised husband and the city-bred wife. We're not just talking different planets here; this man and woman are often from different *solar systems*!

We've muddled our way through many Mars and Venus moments in our 30 years together. One of the earliest involved an 8N Ford tractor; one of the latest, fire; and one still to be resolved, the laundry room.

It's a Man Thing

I have been told and have also observed there are certain tasks and activities couples should not attempt together. Number one on the list seems to be wallpapering. My personal contribution to this list would be "Pull-Starting an 8N Ford Tractor." Definitely not a Mars/Venus collaboration!

One frigid winter day, Bill poked his head in the back door and yelled, "June? June! JUNE!!" Thinking "imminent disaster," I raced from the back of the house. Big mistake! (Note to Self: Next time, yell back "I'm in the bathroom for an extended stay and do not expect to be out until evening.")

"The 8N won't start. Can you come out and help me?" So I threw on my denim farm chore jacket and headed out to the barn. The tractor was chained behind the Ford pickup.

"I put the pickup in four-wheel drive low," he instructed. "Put the gear shift in LOW and pull forward *very slowly* until the chain is tight, then go *very slowly* on out past the barn into the pasture. I'll wave when the tractor starts."

Very slowly. Okey dokey.

Bill hopped on the tractor and I climbed into the truck. I put the gear shift in LOW, that would be to the far right on the PRNDL scale, and *very slowly* pressed on the accelerator. Nothing. I pressed a little harder. Still nothing. "What are you doing? I'm freezing my butt off out here!" One wondered what we were doing out here if it was that cold, but one wisely kept her mouth shut. On the third attempt, I sent about a gallon of gas gushing through the carburetor. The truck lunged forward. I checked the rearview mirror in time to see Bill's head snapping forward on the rebound from having been snapped back. And the air was blue—oh, was it blue! There aren't enough of those little @#%*# characters on the keyboard to begin to cover what was coming out of his mouth!

So we tried again. This time I rationed out enough gas to *very slowly* pull forward and tighten the chain. I checked the mirror again, got a forward wave and *very slowly* proceeded through the gate into the pasture. The tractor roared to life! My job was finished. Bill was all grins and profusely thanked me. No mention of whiplash.

Now, let's take this same scenario and do a *what if* version, as in *what if* I wasn't available to drive the truck and Bill called Neighbor Jim across the road to help. Here's how the Mars/Mars version might play out:

We'll pick it up where Jim pressed on the accelerator to *very slowly* pull forward to tighten the chain. Jim, being a guy, has a heavier foot and gave the truck more gas. The truck leaped forward, jerking the front end of the tractor up in an 8N wheelie. (Okay, I exaggerate!) Bill nearly tumbled off the back of the tractor. He righted himself in the seat and gave a friendly wave to Jim. No blue air and no @#%*#. Jim stuck his head out the window and apologized. "Hey, sorry, man! This Ford accelerator is a lot touchier than the one in my Chevy." Bill laughed and replied, "That's okay! No harm done. Give 'er another go!"

There aren't enough of those little @#%*#! characters on the keyboard to begin to cover what I'm thinking!

From High Heels to Gumboots

Pasture Pyrotechnics

A number of years later, we discovered another farm activity with major potential to create Mars/Venus galactic discord: burning a pasture.

Burning off a pasture in early spring is an effective means of grassland management for several reasons. Burning gets rid of dead grass and weeds left from the previous grazing season, releases nutrients into the ground that revitalize the pasture, helps break the crowns on native grass so they will spread out and kills ticks and parasitic worms. The result in a few weeks is a lush green pasture of nutritious, tender grass the cattle can't wait to sink their teeth into.

The pastures we own or rent all contain 80 acres or less. Bill can usually conduct a burn with three pieces of equipment: the mini-truck, a propane bottle from the gas grill with a hose and torch head, and a water tank with hose and nozzle. The propane bottle sets in the bed of the truck directly behind the driver and the water tank sets beside it. He can stick his arm out the window and hold the torch down toward the ground to set his fire line. Once the burn is over, he can switch to the water hose and douse any remaining hot spots.

Setting a fire outdoors any place other than in a grill requires a burn permit number. The number is issued by the local fire district and identifies us as landowners by name and address. When Bill needs to burn a pasture, he calls the fire dispatcher, gives them his number and asks their blessing to burn.

One early spring evening, Bill made a spur of the moment decision to burn one of our native grass pastures. Conditions were favorable: moderate wind in a direction which would blow the fire toward another one of our pastures and not toward any neighbors; the pasture on the downwind side was green so the fire wouldn't advance beyond the fence line; and, rain was forecast for later in the night.

There was one unfavorable aspect to this plan: Bill had burned other pastures in the last few days and was experiencing soreness in his shoulder from holding the torch, then the water hose, out the window of the mini-truck. He needed a driver so he could sit in the back of the truck and use both arms interchangeably. Hence, the inevitable request: "June! I need your help, please."

"Oh, boy!" I thought, "Mars/Venus fireworks using *real* fire." Remembering the pickup had a dump bed, I issued a warning, "I have a dump lever and I know how to use it!"

Since the wind was blowing out of the southeast, the first task was to set a back-burn strip along the north fence line of the pasture. The purpose of a back-burn strip is to create a burned out area that will stop the pasture fire for lack of fuel when it reaches this strip. The strip is narrow so the back-burn fire is of low intensity and goes out when it reaches the green grass at the fence line.

Once again, my job was to drive *very slowly* in low gear while Bill used his gas bottle torch to set the fire. After a couple of *"Slow down's!"* he directed me to switch to four-wheel drive low. I barely pressed on the accelerator but still got a *"Slow down!"* so I removed my foot from the pedal and just let the truck idle along. We were barely crawling, but apparently this was optimal speed for pasture burning.

We headed west along the north fence and came to a corner where we turned north for a short distance of about 30 yards. I was intensely focused on not accelerating except when absolutely necessary to crawl over a terrace, and maintaining a narrow distance of six feet from the fence. That's about the extent of my multi-tasking ability. Between the focus and the excessive noise level created by the truck engine and the whooshing of the gas bottle torch, along with total hearing loss in my right ear, it's no wonder I couldn't hear Bill yelling, *"GO, GO, GO!"* at the top of his lungs.

I checked the side mirrors to see what the ruckus was about, but both were caked with a mixture of mud and manure. I poked my head out the window and looked back to see Bill with his feet pulled up into the bed of the truck, bright orange flames tickling the bottoms of those feet. He was frantically waving at me to *"GO!"* When we had changed direction and headed north, the southeast wind blew the flames into his feet, which had been hanging out the back of the truck bed. I was literally holding his feet to the fire! Fortunately, no damage occurred to his shoes or feet.

I quickly shifted into neutral, disengaged the four-wheel drive lever and moved it to two-wheel high, shifted back into low gear and managed to pull ahead a few yards without popping the clutch and sending Bill to pasture purgatory. By then we were almost finished with the short northerly stretch so we turned the corner and headed west. I stopped, shifted back into four-wheel drive low and we crawled along at the optimal slower-than-slow pace to finish the back burn.

Once we completed the back-burn, we cruised—finally!—over to the southeast corner of the pasture to start the real pyrotechnics. Setting the fire for the main event worked the same as for the back-burn: creep along while

Bill held the torch close to the ground to ignite the dead grass. I could now gauge wind direction and its affect on flame direction so I knew when to accelerate to avoid barbecuing Bill's feet.

The rest of the burn went fairly well, except for one incident. Bill yelled at me to *"STOP!"* so I did. I leaned out the window and looked back at him. He pointed to a spot he missed and directed me to back up. I looked in the direction he was pointing and saw that to do so, I had to drive through fire. Not a huge wall of flames, maybe only a foot high. But the mini-truck was built fairly low to the ground, which put the gas tank too close to the flames for my comfort level. I thought to myself, "Honey, I know I'm supposed to love you enough to walk through fire, but *driving* through fire in a vehicle with a gas tank just goes above and beyond reasonable expectations." I drove around in a circle until we reached the missed spot. He told me later he drove through flames lots of times. Mental post-it note: Make sure his will is current and his life insurance is paid up.

We completed the burn, doused any remaining hot spots with water, headed to the barn to put away the equipment, then on to the house for relaxing showers to wash away the smoky smell. Bill was pleased he "got a good burn" and I was happy that after more than 25 years, we were finally getting the hang of Mars/Venus compatibility on the farm.

Mars and Venus in the Laundry Room

We have a Mars/Venus issue in the laundry room: Whose responsibility is it to empty the pockets of Bill's clothes prior to being laundered? My contention is it's *his* duty to empty all pockets before the items are tossed in the dirty laundry basket. His contention is it's *my* duty to empty pockets as I put items into the washing machine. Stalemate!

Well, Mars prevailed on this one, so I mumbled and grumbled every time I sorted laundry. Venturing into the abyss of Bill's pockets requires a flashlight and yields a vast array of man flotsam and jetsam, some potentially lethal, which falls into several categories:

Farming: Nuts, bolts, washers, nails, screws, fence staples, rubber bands used in castrating bull calves, valve stem covers, syringe needle covers, seeds, fertilizer pellets, hay, grain, range cubes, dirt mixed with dried manure and some stuff I can't identify.

Hunting: Shotgun and rifle shells, duck and turkey calls, duck stamp. Yes, I washed and dried his duck stamp. But we were able to retrieve

115

enough pieces from the dryer lint filter to convince the Fish and Game people to issue a replacement.

Fishing: This can be scary! Fish hooks, about a hundred different varieties of brightly colored plastic lures and jigs, fly fishing flies, lead weights, dead bait and sometimes, even *live* bait.

Football Officiating: Yellow penalty flag, bean bag used to mark ball spots, yardage clip, game information card, bullet pencil. This last item somehow eludes my pocket search so it's extremely clean!

Miscellaneous: Pocket knife, Chapstick, driver's license, credit cards, ink pens, combs, Post-It notes containing critically important snippets of information, handkerchiefs (most of his white handkerchiefs are now a pretty shade of light blue because they were left in blue jean pockets), and *money!*

You can see why I caved on this issue: some of that stuff could damage *my* clothes not to mention the washer or dryer. However, there is an advantage to pulling pocket-emptying duty: finding money, both coins and bills. If I miss coins in the pocket search, they usually collect in the bottom of the washer. If they don't agitate out of pockets in the washer, then I hear them as they tumble around in the dryer. I can identify the type of coin just by hearing it clank in the dryer.

Paper money launders exceptionally well. The paper stock used for our currency can withstand washing and drying. Unlike the duck stamp, bills do not disintegrate in the laundering process.

My philosophy on finding buried treasure in the laundry room is "Finders, Keepers." I did relent on one occasion and returned a $20 bill. But, dear, take heed: the next one is mine!

Quid Pro Quo on the Farm

Quid Pro Quo—Latin for "You do something for me and I'll do something for you."

On this particular March day, it meant if I hard-boiled eggs for Bill to make deviled eggs for a dinner at his sister's house the next day, he would wash my car. (The former home ec major in me refrained from correcting him: You do not *hard-boil* eggs; you *hard-cook* them.) I had intended to cook the eggs anyway, but I wasn't going to divulge that information and miss the opportunity for a free car wash using someone else's manual labor.

Bill had a busy day planned: a 9:00 a.m. meeting in our neighborhood, noon appointment with our income tax preparer, afternoon delivery of tanks for the new water system in our pastures, and Topeka Officials Association meeting in the evening. Herding six fugitive bred heifers from the brome field back to their designated pasture was *not* on the agenda.

As I was rinsing out my coffee cup at the kitchen sink, I looked out the window and saw the six young ladies grazing their way across the backyard. Bill was in the bathroom shaving. I asked, "Did you leave a gate open when you fed the heifers?"

"Guess I did," was the reply from the half-shaven face. "How many?"

"About six. I'll take care of it."

After 30 years on the farm, I have formed a philosophy about gates: Cattle can't get out through a closed gate. It's simple and doesn't require much in the way of farm smarts to figure out. I already knew which gate was open and how it happened.

This year, Bill kept 10 of his yearling heifers to breed during January and February. Every morning he used the mini-truck to haul a couple of buckets of grain and small bales of hay out of the barn, through the corral pen and into a small pasture near the house. A swinging gate next to the barn led to the pen. To save time and effort, he left this one open all the time. The next gate wasn't actually a gate, but two side-by-side tubular steel fence panels that were part of his corral pen system. Bill got out of his truck and opened one panel to create an opening wide enough to drive through. He left this "gate" open until he was finished feeding, then closed it when he went back to the barn...usually.

Bill's brain had fast-forwarded to the busy day ahead. He drove back through the gap and right on to the barn. No memory rewind warning him to go back and close the opening between the panels. It didn't take long for some of the heifers to find the gap, the open gate next to the barn, then the yard beyond.

I threw on my jacket, stepped into my gumboots, grabbed a small bucket of range cubes from the garage and went out to return those bad girls to the pasture. I didn't anticipate any problems because they were very tame and would ordinarily follow us anywhere if we rattled a bucket of cubes.

I shook the bucket and yelled, "S'calf, s'calf!" The heifers started to follow me, then realized they were returning to the pasture where they had already cropped off part of the new grass and trampled the rest. They changed direction and headed back across the yard.

So the extradition wasn't going to be as easy as I thought. What I hadn't taken into account was the allure of tender, succulent new grass in the yard. A late-February blizzard dropped about a foot of snow, followed by a couple of weeks of mild to warm temperatures and an inch and a half of rain, coaxed new grass to the surface. Furthermore, the heifers' breakfast menu for five months consisted of grain, hay and apple pulp left over from a local apple farm's cider-making operation. What our heifers didn't realize was they were darned lucky to get that apple pulp! Even worse, the last big bale of hay Bill put out for them was of inferior quality and moldy. No wonder they didn't want to go back! For them, new grass in the spring is a highly anticipated treat, just like new asparagus from our garden is for us.

Bill came out of the house and grabbed his herding sticks out of the bed of the mini-truck, which was parked in the driveway. He tried to get around the small herd and redirect them toward the pasture. They knew what that meant and they were having none of it! They continued grazing in a northerly direction toward the empty soybean field.

By this time, four heifers remaining in their home pasture were making their way through the open gate and into the corral pen. From there, they had two options: follow the first bunch through the gate into the yard; or, head the other direction through yet another open gate into the east pasture. Two of the heifers wandered into the yard, but Bill abandoned the other chase to redirect them successfully back into the corral. He sent me to close the gate leading to the east pasture.

With all means of escape secured, we headed back to deal with the original escapees only to find them trotting down the road about half a mile away. We jumped in the mini-truck and raced to intercept them in a bumpy, jarring ride across a field of soybean stubble and into the brome hay meadow. Bill uses the truck to feed, so when the heifers heard the roar of the engine, they changed course and veered into the brome.

If they thought tender, succulent, young fescue shoots were tasty, wait until they chowed down on new brome shoots!

We caught up with the heifers and Bill grabbed a bucket of grain out of the truck bed, shook it and called, "S-calf, s-calf," as he attempted to lead them toward a gate 50 yards away between the brome field and their pasture. They started to follow then apparently decided it was time for another snack. When they discovered the delectable brome shoots, all forward progress stopped. They refused to be denied this unexpected delicacy!

Seeing assistance was needed, I bailed out of the truck and initiated a rear flank herding tactic by making shooing motions with my arms. Bill yelled for me to go back to the truck and get the herding sticks to prod them along. When that didn't work, he again sent me back to the truck, this time to drive behind them, honk the horn and herd them in the general direction of the gate.

What he was asking me to do required a person to have three hands attached to the same number of arms, and an identical arrangement of feet and legs. The hand/arm motions were to steer the truck, honk the horn and shift gears. The foot/leg motions were to operate the clutch, brake and accelerator. These motions were performed in short, high-speed bursts using low gear and reverse, like fast-forwarding then rewinding a DVD several dozen times. The little mini-truck became a mechanical herding dog. But, instead of a dog nipping at the heifers' heels, the grill of the truck nudged their butts. Bill provided the herding commands: "Come on, come on!" "Backup, backup!" "Watch that heifer! She broke for the east fence!" "Go west! Credence is headed for the road!"

Apparently, the heifers realized the Japanese mini-truck, herding with the persistence of a Border Collie, wasn't going to leave them to enjoy their snack in peace. They finally ambled toward Bill and the open gate, occasionally stopping for one last taste. Bill opened the gate and waved them back into their home pasture.

As I followed the last heifer through the gate I stopped and asked, "Did you say you would *detail* my car?!"

June Hilbert

DOMESTICITY ON THE FARM

I once saw a bumper sticker that read, "My Only Domestic Quality is I Live in a House." Hilarious! I wanted to flag down the driver and find out where I could get one. Except that it wouldn't be appropriate for me. As much as I would like to deny my domesticity, it's hard-wired into me. My gene pool is chlorinated with bleach, ammonia and, about a century ago, lye. Environmentalists will be pleased to hear we recently removed the phosphates.

Moving from a one-bedroom condominium in the city to a farm house in the country meant I not only had to quit denying my domesticity, I had to ratchet it up several notches. This discovery created inner conflict that manifested itself as outer bitchiness until I realized...

All Work and No Play Makes June a Very Bitchy Girl!

One of the most difficult farm concepts for me to grasp has been the perpetual work concept. Farm work is never *done*. When one task is complete, another awaits. Furthermore, some tasks are never complete; they are perpetual. My pre-farm philosophy was every project had a definite beginning that progressed logically to a defined end. Not so on the farm. It nearly drove me nuts! To further add to the frustration, I was raised to get my work done before being allowed to go out and play. Applying that principle on the farm meant I would never get any playtime! I had to disconnect from my previous philosophy in order to make the adjustments critical to maintaining my sanity.

One example of my pre-farm philosophy of project beginning/end was housecleaning. I come from a long line of very neat and tidy housekeepers.

Not necessarily meticulous, but neat and tidy. My mother introduced me to every phase of housecleaning and laundry as soon as she decided I was old enough. I washed dishes, vacuumed, scrubbed floors, dusted, cleaned the bathroom, hung laundry on the clothesline, removed laundry from the clothesline, ironed and/or folded and put it away. And all before noon! Just kidding. But, during the summer, whether or not we were allowed to go swimming in the afternoon usually hinged on getting the day's work done.

When I lived in a one-bedroom condominium, house-cleaning had a definite beginning and end, usually separated by only one hour. This included vacuuming, damp-mopping the postage-stamp-sized kitchen floor, dusting a few pieces of furniture and cleaning the bathroom. The goal was to do these chores weekly although it probably wasn't necessary and it didn't always happen weekly.

Then I moved to the farm and the days of one-hour cleaning were over. I now lived in a three-bedroom house with no air conditioning except through open windows, a wood-burning stove in the living room, a man who ranked house-cleaning as low priority, a Golden Retriever and a cat. Talk about dust! And, with all of the outside debris tracked in, I could farm on the kitchen floor! On the upside, there was only one bathroom to clean and, at that time, we did not live on a gravel road. Two years later, we moved to a house on a gravel road and I gained a second bathroom to clean. But this house had central air and we put a wood furnace in the basement. Nevertheless, I came to the realization rural house-cleaning had a beginning, but definitely no end!

My sanity was slipping away like sliding sock-footed across a freshly waxed kitchen floor.

Then I happened to read about another kindred spirit's inner turmoil. Like me, she had a love/hate relationship with house-cleaning: love a clean house but hate to clean it. She made a monumentally profound observation: Did you ever hear a dying woman proclaim with her last breath, "Gee, I wish I had spent more time cleaning house!" Who wants to die and leave a clean house as her only legacy? It was a sanity-saving epiphany!

Since the epiphany, I granted myself permission to dial back the cleaning...somewhat. I still spend a few hours each weekend cleaning and doing laundry, just not as obsessively. I try to keep the clutter at bay. But since Bill retired from his State job and turned to running his cattle operation full-time, the living room resembles the periodical room of a farm library, with cattle and farming publications scattered around. If he's doctoring cows or calves, a large pistol-grip hypodermic needle can be found on the kitchen counter, ready for the next dose of medication. If we're bottle-feeding a calf, a two-quart plastic "baby bottle" complete with large nipple can also be found on the counter.

I am more relaxed about people seeing my house in whatever degree of chaos it's in. My house won't win any awards in *House Beautiful* magazine, and probably not in *Farm and Ranch Beautiful*, if there is one. Heck, some days even honorable mention in *Shack Beautiful* would be a major stretch!

My farm house-cleaning philosophy:

Is the kitchen floor clean enough to eat off of? Not gonna happen!

Is my antique furniture dust-free? What's an antique without a little dust!

Is there dog hair on the couch and recliner? We don't allow the dog on the furniture, but there is dog hair and dander in the house. I can't imagine a life without Golden Retrievers!

That being said, if I ever catch anyone "white-gloving" my house, he or she will be banished from the premises and never invited back!

Feng Shui on the Farm

Feng Shui 101 – Pronounced *fung-SHWAY*. An ancient art and science developed in China over 3,000 years ago, which possibly makes it older than the dirt on my farm. It's a complex body of knowledge aimed at channeling the energy, or *chi*, of any given space for better relationships and greater life balance, harmony and prosperity for those who live in that space.

So, this means feng shui should enhance the farminess of my farm. Right?

As a teenager in the late 1960's and early '70's, I can appreciate the concept of channeling energy to achieve "harmony and understanding, sympathy and trust abounding," which defined the "Age of Aquarius" as sung by the *5th Dimension*. We channeled energy by hanging psychedelic posters in our bedrooms; painting peace signs on everything from T-shirts to Volkswagens; and wearing brightly colored beads to proclaim our love of all mankind.

Then there was the dark side of the "Age of Aquarius": Those who sought to align Jupiter with Mars by channeling the energy of hallucinogenic substances through their veins. Though not as prevalent in the Midwest Bible Belt as it was in San Francisco's Haight-Ashbury district, seeking the "mind's true liberation" using chemical means still existed. But the closest I ever got to acid was in chemistry class, where we quickly learned that "dropping acid" would burn holes in our clothes and shoes. Not an advisable way to "let the sun shine in."

Now, some 40-plus years later, as a middle-aged farm wife, how do I channel energy in my home away from *Little House on the Prairie Meets the Funny Farm* and toward better relationships, greater life balance, harmony and prosperity? Oh yeah, especially prosperity.

According to my research, getting started with feng shui was easy when you start with the house basics and gradually move on to the more complex levels. Those must be the barns, machine shed, chicken house, tool shed, grain storage buildings and outhouse. Can't wait to learn how to channel energy and attain greater life balance, harmony and prosperity in the outhouse!

The basic feng shui steps are:

1. Clear Out the Clutter—This is critical. Do not skip this step. You can't have a harmonious house amid clutter. It places road blocks in the energy path and energy doesn't do detours. *Of course, this means I'm in trouble already because I HATE to clean.*

2. Have Good Quality Air and Light—Fresh air and abundant natural light are essential for good feng shui energy. Open the windows to clear out house smog. *Living on a gravel road and opening the windows to let in the fresh air guarantees a layer of dust settles on everything. The windows let in some natural light, but I wouldn't call it abundant. And, since we converted to those new compact fluorescent light bulbs, the house seems dim. We may be saving energy and money, but I doubt they promote good feng shu.*

3. Define the *Bagua*, or the feng shui energy map of your house. *Heck, that's easy—just follow the carpet traffic patterns to determine the energy flow in my house!* Once the bagua is identified, you will know which areas of your home are connected to specific areas of your life. Example: The southeast feng shui area of the home is connected to the flow of money energy. *Oh really? Well, my recliner is in the southeast corner of my home and so far, I don't feel money energy flowing into my lap while I'm sitting there.*

4. Use the five basic feng shui elements—wood, fire, earth, metal and water—to create balance and energy in all areas of the home. *We have plenty of wood: house, furniture and wood for the wood furnace. In winter, there is fire in the wood furnace and I really don't want it any place else. There is plenty of earth on the kitchen floor, enough to grow crops. On laundry day, I find plenty of metal—nails, screws, nuts, bolts, and coins—in the bottom of the washer. If I don't find them there, they clang around in the dryer. The water*

in my home flows out of the faucets and into sinks, tub, shower and washing machine. I don't want it coming from above or circulating throughout the house. And toilet water circulating through the house is a disaster!

5. Determine your personal feng shui birth element—wood, fire, earth, metal or water—and use it in your home to nourish and support your energy. *I have no idea how to determine my feng shui birth element, but one website offered to help me with that for 67.00 Canadian dollars.*

6. Learn your *kua* number, which is calculated based on gender and date of birth. This number will help you determine your lucky feng shui direction. *American math is all I can handle; I'm not taking on Chinese numbers and I have no clue how to operate an abacas. And lucky direction? Is that an oxymoron? With my sense of direction, I can get lost in my own backyard!*

7. Be aware of the feel of your home and how its energy affects your well-being by being aware of how the feng shui trinity—bedroom, bathroom and kitchen—affects your health. *No problem, I spend most of my time in those three rooms.*

Okay, obviously there are major obstacles to my quest for greater life balance, harmony and prosperity using feng shui. So, for the present, my life will remain lopsided, off-tune and working class.

"Oh good!" Bill exclaimed as he looked over my shoulder when I was researching feng shui on the Internet. "We're having Chinese for supper!" Obviously, he confused "shui" with "suey," as in chop suey.

"No, dear. Don't crack open that bottle of soy sauce yet. I'm researching *feng shui*, an ancient Chinese art and science that teaches people how to arrange their homes to channel positive energy, thereby achieving balance, harmony and prosperity.

"What's wrong with this house? It looks and feels just fine to me and I'm happy here. Why get the Chinese involved?"

Huge sigh! "So I can sit in the southeast corner of our home in my recliner and have tons of money pour down on me."

Huge sigh! That one was Bill's.

Man Cave Feng Shui in the Barn

Even though Bill had no idea what feng shui was and no grasp of the concept, he channeled his farm energy to create a peaceful, harmonious space for himself in one corner of our new barn. It is his man cave. Or, as my brother and several people commented during a tour of the new barn when Bill showed them his workshop, "This is the dog house!" The presence of amenities—microwave oven, dorm-size refrigerator, and sacks of feed stacked on a pallet, which could be converted into a make-shift bed— give this space the appearance of a rustic efficiency apartment.

Whether the space is a man cave or a dog house depends on perspective. From Bill's perspective, the space is a man cave where he seeks refuge from bad energy in the house, a cranky wife. A visit to the man cave restores his life's peace and harmony, while it allows cranky wife to fumigate the bad energy out of the house. This rebalancing of the house energy promotes greater understanding in the relationship and prosperity: the assets remain intact versus being divided in half.

From my perspective, the space is a dog house where farmer-under-foot is banished, kind of like a time-out, as I cling precariously to my last nerve. I sweep the bad energy out after him, which has great restorative power for my peace and harmony. Then, the house energy rebalances, promoting greater understanding, and prosperity doesn't become an ugly issue.

Actually, the man cave/dog house has a utilitarian function: it really is a workshop. Bill built a workbench in one corner with pegboard on the walls above it to hang up tools. There are metal cabinets along two walls for storage. The small refrigerator provides cool storage for the vaccines, antibiotics and other medications necessary to maintain healthy cattle. The microwave is a convenience in case he wants to heat up something to eat or drink. The pallet of feed sacks is stored in this room because, unlike the rest of the barn, it has a concrete floor so the feed stays drier than if it was stored on a pallet on the ground.

I hate to admit it, but someone who doesn't know feng shui from chop suey channeled the energy in his space to create better relationships and greater life balance, harmony and prosperity than I did in the house. I'm still stuck at *Little House on the Prairie Meets the Funny Farm!*

Farm Fashion

Remember Eva Gabor as the Upper Manhattan bejeweled fashion plate socialite-turned-farm-wife on the 1960's TV comedy *Green Acres*? I still have a mental picture of her dressed in the frilly negligee and peignoir set with matching stiletto-heeled mules, diamond earrings dangling from her ears, climbing up the telephone pole to answer the ringing phone. "*O-lee-vah! It's fah youuu!!*" or cooking "hotscakes" for Oliver's breakfast.

From High Heels to Gumboots

Haute couture on the farm is not Dior, Valentino or Prada. It is Carhartt, Lee for Women or Northerner. Country singer Gretchen Wilson put it quite succinctly in "Redneck Woman" when she sang she didn't shop for underwear at Victoria's Secret because she could buy the "same damn thing" at Wal-mart a lot cheaper. I probably would not recommend wearing a thong and "Wonder Bra" to do farm chores; but then, I haven't tried it.

My current denim farm chore jacket is a $5.00 garage sale purchase from 15 years ago. It was styled up a bit to appeal to the young, fashionable female market of about 20 years ago, but it's still very "serviceable" (an adjective used frequently to describe farm apparel) and in great condition. Another indispensible piece of winter outerwear I would recommend for anyone living on a Kansas farm and points north is a heavy, three-quarter length, olive drab army coat, vintage mid-60's—with or without a cannabis patch sewn on the sleeve. (Those Army Security Agency guys were a wild lot!). Bill had two such coats from his army stint in Germany. I wear one of these army-surplus-hand-me-downs on our evening walks in the winter.

I also own a pair of gumboots, a/k/a muck boots, sized for women. These boots are an absolute must-have for every on-the-go farm wife, particularly when on-the-going involves slogging through a corral full of mud and cow manure to feed cattle. I call these my "Big Girl Boots."

Decked out in Bill's ragged-around-the-edges army coat and Cargill Industries freebie stocking cap, my own heavy work gloves and olive drab gumboots, I've created a distinctive fashion statement: *Farm Wife Barbie meets Army Surplus Refugee.*

This isn't to say farm wives can't or don't want to look stylish. None of us wants to be tagged as a "frumpy farm wife" or an "ag hag" by our "city slicker sisters." Many of us have part- or full-time jobs off the farm, so we do mingle with the general public and keep up with current fashion. And, most of us do enjoy at least an occasional shopping trip to retailers other than Tractor Supply or Orscheln Farm Store.

At my day job at the bank in Topeka, there is a dress code. Although it has relaxed somewhat in recent years, the "approved apparel" list still doesn't include denim farm chore jackets, army surplus coats promoting illegal substances or gumboots. My closet space is filled with conservative suits, skirts, slacks, blouses and corporate logo polo shirts. My dresser drawers are full of jeans, T-shirts, chambray and flannel shirts, warm socks, gloves and long underwear.

I don't have to travel very far to catch the new spring collection at Tractor Supply or "Denim Daze" at Orscheln Farm Store. Nor do I need a passport. Maybe I'll see you there!

I'm Not Having a Hot Flash—We're Burning Hedge!

In our basement squats a big hulking, smoke-belching, black behemoth: the wood furnace.

When I met Bill, he lived in a little old farmhouse on 10 acres. The main heat source was a small wood stove in the living room. He had a "real" furnace of the forced-air gas variety that he used sparingly, mainly first thing in the morning to start heating the house while he built a fire in the wood stove. Not since I was very young had I experienced wood heat. Natural gas came to my hometown when I was about five years old and, since then, any place I lived had either an electric or gas furnace.

I quickly learned several things about wood stove heat: It wasn't consistent heat, and the front of the house where the stove was located was very warm while the bedrooms were very cool. Once a fire was started, it was necessary to continue feeding wood into the stove to sustain the heat. If the fire burned out during the night, the house was pretty darn chilly in the morning.

A wood stove does not burn clean. There was always the faint odor of smoke in the house. Hauling ashes out of the house and hauling wood into the house through the kitchen into the living room greatly contributed to the general dustiness of country living.

I tolerated the dirt and dust for about two years after we were married. Then, we mutually agreed to start looking for another farm. Bill wanted more land and I wanted a newer house closer to Topeka...and no wood stove. We found a 40-acre farm with an eight-year-old house less than a half-hour from downtown Topeka. The first time we looked at the house I walked into the living room and there sat a wood stove in front of the fireplace. Uh-uh. No!

We eventually bought the place but requested the owners take the wood stove with them. Bill did some research, found a wood furnace and had it installed in the basement. With the basement door located just inside the back door from the garage into the kitchen, the trail of debris was confined to the garage, in the back door and down the stairs to the basement. Twenty-one years later, we moved to our current farm and put a wood furnace in that basement. But this house had a unique feature: a concrete "safe room" in the basement with a hatch in the garage floor. We loaded wood in the bed of the mini-truck, backed it into the garage right up to the hatch and dropped the wood down into the safe room.

The difference between a wood stove and a wood furnace is the heat from a wood stove radiates from the stove itself. The heat is not channeled into ductwork to be distributed throughout the house. However, a blower fan can be attached to the stovepipe to push warm air beyond the area around the stove. A wood *furnace* has an interior firebox that is encased within a steel cabinet. Ductwork is attached to the steel cabinet and joined into the existing ductwork in the house. An electric fan on the furnace blows the hot air through the ductwork and up through floor registers. There is a separate stovepipe attached to the firebox for the smoke to exit up through a chimney.

Building fires in either the wood stove or wood furnace was initially scary for me. My only fire-building experience was in Girl Scouts. Since campfires were outdoor activities, the worst-case scenario was burning down someone's timber. Building a fire in my *home* was another matter.

Bill patiently taught me how to lay a fire, starting with balled up newspaper as tinder, adding small sticks of wood as kindling, then larger sticks until a good fire was going; then finally adding logs. Yes, I know: a Girl Scout would be stripped of her badges and dishonorably discharged if caught using newspaper to start a fire. But we weren't earning merit badges; we were trying to start a fire to heat up a freezing house.

We have an indispensable little safety device attached to the stovepipe: a thermometer. It registers the temperature of the air leaving the firebox and exiting up the stovepipe. The round dial has two rings of calibrations: The first ring, which is nearest the edge of the dial, is calibrated by 100s of degrees. The second ring is an explanatory aid for anyone who can't figure out what the optimal temperature for a fire should be. This calibration is called Stovepipe Zones and is divided into three categories: **Creosote** (green), **Best Operation** (yellow), **Too Hot** (red). These zones correspond to the numeric degrees.

The object is to build a fire hot enough to generate sufficient heat so the little pointer passes through the **Creosote** zone quickly and settles into the **Best Operation** zone without red-lining into the **Too Hot** zone. I probably don't need to elaborate on the outcome if the little pointer zips up to **Too Hot** and stays there. If that occurs, the frantic response is to shut off the valve which regulates airflow into the firebox and turn the fan speed up to High.

129

Within a few minutes, the pointer should drop back into the **Best Operation** zone. If not, call 911 and evacuate the premises.

On the other hand, building a fire that heats up slowly, allowing the little pointer to linger in the **Creosote** zone, may also have disastrous results. Building a fire that smolders and smokes excessively will, over time, cause a build-up of creosote, a highly flammable black tarry residue, in the chimney. If enough creosote builds up, the result could be a pyrotechnic extravaganza erupting from the chimney. Then, the house burns down.

There are two ways to procure wood to burn: buy it already cut or cut it yourself. We do the latter. Bill owns two chainsaws and a log splitter; we have a ready supply of timber around us. The wood varieties available include oak, walnut, mulberry, elm, hackberry, hickory and hedge. Of these varieties, hedge is the hottest burning wood. Throw a few small logs of hedge in the fire and the house heats up fast. But keep an eye on that stovepipe thermometer; it *will* red-line in a hurry.

Our tinder of choice, newspaper, is also readily available, most of the time. We burn every type of newspaper we can get our hands on, from the county *Weekly Wipe* to the *Wall Street Journal.* (*Weekly Wipe* was the nickname given to the once-a-week newspaper in my hometown by those residents old enough to remember the days before indoor plumbing and toilet tissue.) If we do run low on newspaper? Well, there's always dumpster-diving at the recycling center. Don't laugh—Bill really did that!

The point of heating with wood is to save money. Propane, like all petroleum products, has become hideously expensive and we probably haven't seen the worst yet. I've observed the propane delivery man make so many trips to some of our neighbors he's considered one of the family.

I'm still a turn-the-dial-on-the-thermostat kind of gal. It's so simple: when you want heat, you turn up the thermostat and the "real" furnace kicks on. I don't need a lot of heat, 68-70 degrees suits me just fine. However, the cost of filling up a 1,000-gallon propane tank once a month for about five months doesn't suit my budget. So we fill the belly of the big hulking, smoke-belching, black behemoth, strike a match and wait for the little flame to ignite into a roaring conflagration which creates the blessed heat to warm our home.

No, I'm not having a hot flash—we're burning hedge!

FUN AND GAMES ON THE FARM

I discovered farm entertainment can happen spontaneously and can involve events or situations that never, in my wildest City Girl dreams, would I have ever thought could be fun and just plain hilarious.

Farm Federation Tag Team Rat Smack-Down

One of those events occurred when Bill was away on an overnight work trip. I took the usual evening walk in the pasture to check cattle with our two Goldens: Ginger, the older dog, and Brandy, the two-year-old. As usual, the exuberant Brandy raced back to the barn ahead of us. When Ginger and I arrived, we found her in a stock tank, which was half full of grain for the cattle, frantically chasing something and whining. Ginger charged up to the tank and pranced around, desperately wanting a piece of the action, whatever it was. But she was too old and arthritic to jump into the tank and too heavy for me to lift. So, much to her great disappointment, she would just have to be a spectator.

Brandy captured the as yet unidentified quarry and immediately flung it out of the tank. I stepped closer to see what it was...*a rat!* Now, you're probably thinking I raced from the barn, hysterically screaming, like any self-respecting City Girl. Not so. I had already learned that mice and rats are relatively harmless and a fact of life on the farm.

Thrilled that she could now participate, Ginger pounced on the rat and gleefully shook it to death. Meanwhile, Brandy was on the hunt for another victim. She scored, then launched it out of the tank and it landed at my feet. The rat didn't move. Good, it's dead. But suddenly, its little feet twitched, it sprang up and scurried to safety under the hay bales. I looked over at

Brandy, glowering at me with her lips curled up in what we called her disgusted expression. "What?" I asked her. She still looked disgusted. "You think *I* let it get away? You could have killed it, you know." Then I remembered she had once been bitten on the nose by a rat she caught and didn't instantly kill. Thereafter, whenever she chased a rodent, she would chomp on it and immediately fling it away before it could bite her. So she was disgusted with me because I didn't finish off her catch.

Then it hit me (a thought, not a rat): *tag team rat smack-down*. I'm in! But first I needed to find a weapon to smack with. A quick search around the barn netted a short-handled shovel. That ought to do it.

Meanwhile, Brandy was racing around inside the tank in hot pursuit of another rat. She caught it, flung it in a high arc, and when it crash-landed, Ginger pounced and dispatched it to rat heaven. Brandy flushed out another victim and sent it soaring. *Incoming!* This one landed at my feet and I walloped it with my shovel for an easy kill. *Dead!* High fives all around! (Well, not really.)

The next rat missile hit my thigh. "Hey, watch it!" Though I don't live in mortal fear of rats, I still don't want to touch them, or have them touch me, even if they are stunned. This one bounced off my thigh, hit the ground running and found temporary asylum in a pile of empty feed sacks. Ginger raced over to the pile and started tearing it apart. I was afraid she wouldn't find the little escapee before it fled so I stomped on the sacks for a few seconds, then peeled them off the pile one at a time. I picked up the last sack and found the fugitive smashed flat.

We continued this rat smack-down frenzy until Brandy couldn't dig up any more victims. Using the shovel, I gathered up the carnage; the death toll stood at six. Not a bad night's work. Now I had to figure out what to do with the little corpses. If I buried them, both dogs would dig them up and play with them. When they became bored with that and the smell became so bad it would gag a maggot, both dogs would roll in the mess. What is it that draws dogs to roll in dead animal matter?!

The best temporary answer was to put the dead rats in a communal body bag, an empty feed sack, and put it up in the bed of Bill's farm truck. The bed was too high for either dog to jump up. Then, when Bill returned home, I would let him dispose of the carnage.

Bill arrived the next evening and I showed him the result of the killing spree. His face registered disbelief, then he laughed. He couldn't believe I had been a participant in a rat-killing game. His comment was, "I wish I had a video of the whole thing!"

Actually, it's probably fortunate there is no video. Although it may be hysterically funny, it might also lead some to question my sanity. That being said, Brandy, Ginger and I had a heckuva good time killing rats in our Farm Federation Tag Team Rat Smack-Down!

Cow Pie Frisbee

I've learned that cow pies are for more than just stepping in.

Bill loves to go to the State Fair in Hutchinson, Kansas, in September. Me? Not so much. I've gone with him a few times. Some of the exhibits were interesting and I enjoyed the musical shows. As a kid, I loved carnival rides. But as an adult? Not so much. As I sat at the very top of the double ferris wheel while it's stopped to load people into a car at the very bottom of the lower wheel, I would find myself obsessing about whether or not a carnival worker tightened all the nuts and bolts. There's this vision in my head of being on the upper wheel as it swoops downward when suddenly it pops out of the frame and careens wildly down the midway.

One evening after Bill had been to the fair, we set out on our evening walk. While he chatted about what he had seen and done at the fair, he walked over to a couple of cow pies, leaned over and peered intently at them. Whenever we suspected the dog had worms, we verified it by checking her manure for the little white parasites. So this intent scrutiny of cow pies didn't seem odd. But when he walked over to another pie and, after a visual examination, poked at it with his finger, I had to ask, "What in the world are you doing?"

"Looking for a good one for you to throw," he answered.

Huh?

Then he explained: The previous day at the fair was proclaimed "Red Hat Society Day" and one of the events planned for the ladies was a cow pie throwing contest. Bill watched as the ladies, attired in their signature purple outfits topped off by distinctive bright red hats, gathered around a wagon loaded with dried-up cow pies. Some contestants approached the selection process with a chorus of *Eewww's* and *Yuk's*. Others dived right in, anxious to grab what they hoped was aerodynamic excrement. Bill noticed one lady in particular, poking her finger gently into the center of several prospective missiles of manure until she found one that met with her approval. He walked over and asked about her selection criteria. She willingly shared her strategy: Select a pie with a slightly soft, but not gooey, center. A finger poked into the center should leave a shallow impression.

Bill joined the gathering crowd of spectators in the contest arena as the red-hatted throwers lined up, ready to hurl their disks of dung. The ladies used a variety of throwing techniques: overhand baseball pitch, underhand softball pitch, discus throw complete with whirling around in a circle, Frisbee toss, or just flinging it out there any way you can and hope for the best. First place went to the lady with the slightly soft-centered pie, with a distance of 15 yards.

So now, using the winner's selection strategy, Bill selected a cow pie for me to throw. As he handed it to me, I contemplated my best throwing technique. Truthfully, I'm not proficient at *any* throwing technique. As I hefted the pie in my hand, the disk shape seemed best suited to a Frisbee technique, despite the fact I've seldom played Frisbee. I grabbed the pie around the rim, bent my elbow and wrist inward and with a quick outward snap, launched my fecal Frisbee. It soared, gaining altitude until it leveled off into a plateau, floated aloft for a few moments, then began a drifting descent to the ground, completing a near-perfect rainbow arch.

Bill stepped off the distance: 20 yards. I could have won first prize!

Maybe I'll buy a big red hat and go to the State Fair!

Splish-Splashing on the Farm

One year, in late winter/early spring, when we lived on our 40-acre farm, Mother Nature dumped a cold, wet one on us: six inches of wet snow. The next day, the temperature rose into the 40s and the big melt-down was on. Bill was gone for a few days on a work-related trip to Oregon. We had no cattle on the place.

What could possibly go wrong? Well, let me tell you...

I came home from work one evening and put on my usual winter evening walking clothes: jeans, turtle-neck shirt, thick socks, heavy army coat, stocking cap, gloves and fleece-lined snow boots. The evening was warmer than I anticipated, so I was a little over-dressed.

A drainage creek meandered through our property. Since our place on the south side of the road was lower than our neighbor's place on the north side of the road, their run-off flowed through a tube under the road and emptied into our drainage creek. The creek was flowing swiftly, except where leaves, sticks and other debris dammed it up. I noticed this as Brandy and I started our walk.

We slogged and sloshed through the pasture. I had over-dressed and, due to all that slogging and sloshing, warmed up quickly. I took off the stocking cap and gloves, stashed them in a pocket, and unfastened my coat.

As we neared the end of our walk, I realized I wasn't yet ready to go to the house. It was one of those March evenings when you realize, yes, spring was almost here and you just want to savor the feeling. As we crossed the creek, I flashed back to when I was a kid, and I played with my siblings and friends in the rain-swollen ditches in front of our house. What a blast!

Regressing back to my childhood, I found a long, sturdy stick and started working my way along the creek bank, breaking up the little dams to release the backed-up water. In some places, the creek was shallow enough I could wade in and kick the dams of debris apart. But for the most part, the water was over my boot tops so I used my stick to merrily flail away at the impediments.

Working my way down the creek, I came to a small waterfall—the drop was only about two feet and the water was muddy. Hardly an idyllic, picturesque scene! Nevertheless, my mission was to eliminate the blockage. And this was a serious blockage; there were major tree branches to remove. My sturdy stick was no match for these branches. There happened to be a small tree on the bank by the waterfall so I was able to wrap one arm around the tree, lean out over the creek, then grab an end of a branch and drag it out of the water. Somewhat precarious, but it worked. So I tried it again, dragging out another branch. The removal of the two branches was enough to dislodge the remaining debris, and it flowed over the waterfall. I levered myself back onto the bank and continued down the creek searching for the next obstruction.

The next dam was on the opposite side of the creek and there was nowhere shallow enough to cross over. But, there was a tree on my side with exposed roots along the bank that made a handy, if somewhat narrow, little platform I could perch on. I stepped down on the first root but it wasn't close enough to the water. I stepped down to the next, and final, root. I settled into a squat position, grabbed the root above me with one hand, leaned out over the creek and flailed at the obstruction with my sturdy stick. What happened next was a blur then and is still a blur now.

I fell in. Head first. I don't know exactly how it happened. Obviously, I leaned out over the creek too far, but I had no awareness of whether my hand slipped off the root or a foot slipped off the root I was crouched on. Since I took a header, I tend to think my hand must have slipped. I just suddenly realized I was under water, very cold water, and could not get my feet under me to stand up. One foot was caught in the tree root. A few moments and a couple of gulps of dirty creek water later, my foot finally came free and I was able to stand up. Luckily, the water was only knee-deep. Whew!

First, and most important, I checked to see if the neighbors were out in their yard, laughing their butts off at me. No audience in sight. They were probably inside the house hiding behind the curtains, laughing their butts off at me. I waded over to the bank, climbed up and sloshed to the house. I was soaked to the skin with cold, dirty creek water, and my boots were full. The old army coat felt like it weighed about a hundred pounds and any pocket that didn't have holes in it was full of water. My gloves and stocking cap were still in one pocket and they were also soaked.

When I finally reached the house, I struggled out of the boots, emptied out a substantial amount of the creek, then went in the back door and straight down to the basement. Stripping down to my underwear, I hung the dripping clothes on a clothesline, except for the coat, which was so heavy I couldn't lift it up. After a hot shower, I would come back down and start a fire in the wood furnace. Maybe everything would be dry in about a week.

Now for that hot shower! I couldn't resist taking a quick look in the mirror, which was a big mistake. My hair was plastered to my head, full of little twigs, bits of dried leaves and mud. Thirty minutes, 40 gallons of hot water and a half bottle of shampoo later, I was my old fastidious self.

What possesses a 40-something year old woman who wears suits and an every-hair-in-place hairdo to her professional office job, to cavort at the edge of a cold, dirty creek?!

CARS, SEX AND COUNTRY ROADS

The title of this essay might suggest I'm about to reveal the lurid details of my high school dating life. Heh, heh...nope! This piece of Farm Fresh Filosophy is about the *other* love affairs of my life, those involving four wheels and a transmission, and how country roads have sullied those beloved objects of my affection.

Caution: May contain some graphic technical automotive material not suitable for women who subscribe to the theory, *If it has tires or testicles, you're going to have trouble with it.*

Please be patient, ladies. I'm just throwing out a few crumbs to the testosterone-endowed crowd.

Along with throwing in the towel—and dust rag—on keeping a spotless house, I also threw in the chamois on keeping a spotless car. With the exception of the farm at Valley Falls, which was located on a secondary highway, we've lived on gravel roads. The roads are dusty when dry and muddy when wet.

I learned early that taking my car to the Car Spa to luxuriate in the full treatment could put a huge dent in my life's savings. Once I arrived home, it looked as dirty as it did before the trip. We own a small power washer, which is great for quick cleanups. But when I need to strip off a couple of layers of serious road scum, I buy a roll of quarters and head for the do-it-yourself car wash. I usually come home with about a third of the roll left.

My assigned parking stall at work was in the basement of the parking garage, along with most of the other officers of the bank. I guiltlessly parked my dusty/muddy Chevy Malibu among the immaculately shiny Mercedes, Audi's, BMW's and Lexi of the senior officers. There are other officers further down the food chain who drive lower profile vehicles and most of those are still cleaner than my car. But then, I doubt if anyone can match me for furthest commuter miles driven on gravel roads.

Besides the dust and mud, the gravel itself violates the integrity of a car's windshield, paint and tires. Following a vehicle too closely or meeting one intent on breaking the sound barrier turns loose gravel into missiles of mass destruction, chipping glass and paint.

Tires have a shorter life expectancy when run on gravel roads. The incidences of flat tires increase exponentially from hazards like sharp pieces of gravel, nails, screws, broken beer bottles and pointed objects which fall from or break off farm equipment. I even ran over a handle-less screw driver and ruined a tire.

Gravel devours tire tread. Most standard passenger car tires wear out quicker when subjected regularly to gravel roads. The tires on my '99 Cougar were a special design and size commissioned by Mercury from a major tire manufacturer. I had to replace them after 20,000 miles and only three companies produced that size, which made them fairly expensive. Ouch!

My first car was a 1968 Dodge Charger purchased in 1975 when I moved to Topeka and started working full-time—that third part of the "get-a-job, get-an-apartment, get-a-car" trilogy. It was one of the classic muscle cars, not the super righteous 440 four-barrel carburetor Magnum R/T model, but a very respectable 383 two-barrel. That car didn't just have horsepower...it had 0-to-60 *virility!* Even though it had an automatic transmission, the gearshift was on the floor anointing me as dominatrix of that raw, virile power even if I couldn't shift through the gears. I was proud of that car and worshipfully washed and waxed it by hand.

During my Charger love affair, another love entered my life, this one a guy who also happened to be a mechanic. Love me, love my Charger, and he did. But the marriage didn't last—the human one.

One of the gut-wrenching decisions to be made was whether I wanted to keep my Charger or take the new, economical Subaru station wagon we had purchased. Sadly, practicality won out over sentimentality: I took the Subaru and gave up custody of the Charger to the soon-to-be-ex. Because it was almost 12 years old, the car could have easily become a mechanical liability for me. He would give it a good home and attend to its mechanical needs. But, dang! I wish I still had that car!

For the next 12 years, I drove small, economical station wagons, either Subaru or Nissan. The little wagons were good, dependable transportation, nothing more. There was no exhilarating driving experience, no emotional attachment, just a mode of transportation. Keeping them clean was now a chore of drudgery, not a gesture of affection. During this time, I met and married Bill and my work commute changed from city streets to highways and dusty gravel roads. I tried to keep my cars clean, I really did, and still waxed them by hand twice a year. But I couldn't spend all my time and quarters at the car wash.

Then two of my friends bought sporty cars. I was envious. I was bored with nondescript, practical vehicles and missed the sheer joy of being at one with my ride. My life needed a major dose of *pizzazz* administered by fuel injection. The result was a bright red Nissan 240SX with a five-speed manual transmission. (Bright red, as in the color of lipstick my mother never let me wear!) My boss called it "pure, unadulterated sex!" Due to my budgetary constraints, it wasn't Nissan's top of line sports model, but it was sleek, zippy and fun to drive. It had rear-wheel drive, so wasn't practical in snow and ice; but I managed to keep it out of the ditches and away from other drivers' bumpers and fenders.

Sports car infatuation is a lusty, sensuous ride. There is foreplay: the breathless anticipation of slipping into the driver's seat, caressing the steering wheel; a slight catch of breath as you ease the key into the ignition; the sensuous murmur of the engine as it responds to your touch. The *carnal* tension builds and presses you deep into the seat as you finesse the gearshift from first...to second...to third...to fourth...and finally, in a clutch of orgasmic release...*fifth gear*.

Darn! Steamed up the windows again!

Owning a sleek, shiny piece of automotive bling comes with a responsibility: the owner is expected to keep it sleek and shiny, regardless of the dust from gravel roads. I was even taken to task by one of the senior officers at work when I allowed too much dust to accumulate on my car. "If I had a cute sports car like that one, I'd wash it every day," he criticized. He had a Mercedes and it always looked clean. So, when I wasn't at home or at work, I was at the car wash. And I still waxed and buffed out the 240SX by

I put almost 100,000 miles on that little sexpot, partly because none of the automakers had released any newer, sporty models that made me drool. Then, in 1999, Mercury came out with a redesigned Cougar that screamed *attitude* from the grill to the spoiler. I selected a silver one because the dust wouldn't show until it was several layers thick. My Cougar and I prowled around the countryside, shifting gears and having a blast until some gal ran a

139

stop sign in North Topeka and totaled it for me. Fortunately, neither of us was seriously injured.

Once again, I was car shopping but I felt a change niggling its way into my life. That niggling change had a name: practicality. Oh no, please, not an *old lady car*! I envisioned a four-door sedan with automatic transmission, sluggish handling through curves and a body the color of dirt. My sports car persona was screaming, "I'm too young to die! Do this and you'll never have fun again. You'll never feel the road hug of taking a 40-mile-an-hour curve at 60. You'll never win another stoplight drag race. With an automatic transmission, you'll have nothing to do with your hands. You may as well take up crocheting while you drive!"

My sporty persona had a point.

I considered a compromise: sleek design, smoother ride, five-speed manual trannie preferred—but would accept automatic—in silver or light metallic blue that wouldn't show dust. Most of the cars with those features cost a little more than I was prepared to pay, even with the insurance settlement. Speaking of which, the other driver's insurance company finally declared the current love of my life a total loss and gave me three days to find a car before they cut the cord on my free rental car.

After much online research and soul searching, we found another Cougar: a 2002, which was the last model year because Mercury was terminating its production. This one had an automatic transmission (guess I'd be taking crochet lessons) and the color was burgundy, so it would look like a dust-magnet. Mercury tweaked the suspension to smooth out the ride, but sacrificed some of the handling ability. I would be forced to back off to 50 miles per hour on the curves. I was entering the twilight of my sports car years.

My aging Baby Boomer body began to voice its displeasure with my refusal to grow up. The Cougar's low-slung profile may have looked cool but climbing up and out of the thing was beginning to torque my middle-aged joints. Getting in and out of the car was even more difficult for Bill who had to resort to contortionist moves. Even though Mercury softened the suspension, it was still a rough ride. Whenever new gravel was dumped on the roads, the ride would nearly jar my fillings loose. The Cougar ride was also noisy. The doors and windows were not tight and let in too many decibels of road noise, as well as dust. I was irritable and critical of the shortcomings of my beloved car. What was wrong with me?

With a shock, I realized I was entering automotive menopause: a mid-life crisis that occurs when a sports car driver realizes that comfort takes priority over cool. It's like trading the sexy nightie for the flannel pajamas.

I resigned myself to searching for an *old lady car.* Then I happened to read an article about the redesigned Chevy Malibu. In my mind, the Malibu was Chevy's muscle car of the mid- to late-1960s. A true sports car enthusiast would never settle for a lame retro attempt. But, as I researched reviews, my gut feeling was, "This is *my* car." Yes, it was a four-door sedan with automatic transmission. But the styling was upbeat, with a modified fast-back rear profile, minimal interior road noise, smooth ride and ergonomically-friendly seat design. I bought one. The bill of sale listed the color as amber. I think of it as *dusty* amber.

If the bright red Nissan 240SX was my five-speed orgasm-mobile infatuation, then my Chevy Malibu is the comfortable, stable, mature love-of-my-life.

June Hilbert

REALLY GROSS FARM AND PET STUFF

NOTE: If you are eating while you read this or are easily grossed out, you may want to skip the next section.

No doubt about it, living on a farm means encountering some really gross stuff, most of which goes way beyond just stepping in a cow pie. Furthermore, you don't have to come in direct contact with the gross stuff; observing something or someone else dealing with it can also turn your stomach. When I regaled co-workers with my farm experiences, mothers who dealt admirably with all the gross stuff that comes out of babies and young children would go pale just listening to any story involving animal grossities. (Spell Check just red-lined "grossities." So what if I made it up. I like it and it stays!)

LAST WARNING: See NOTE above. If you can't eat while watching *CSI*, then do not proceed beyond this point! Remember, you were warned!

Cattle

In previous chapters, I related some experiences that included encounters with gross stuff.

In "Blessed Events," intervention by pulling a calf became necessary when the natural birthing process went haywire. Any time this happens, it guarantees the CFM (Certified Farm Midwife), a/k/a Bill, will get covered with everything that comes out of the back end of the cow: birth gunk and sometimes pee and poop. The CFMA (Certified Farm Midwife Assistant), me, usually escapes most of it.

The bonding experience of a cow and her newborn calf provides more grossities. The cow gives her calf its first bath by licking off the birth slime.

Then, at some point, the cow eats the afterbirth, an act known as placentophagia. According to some experts, the cow eats afterbirth as a bonding act with her calf. Other experts argue placentophagia is not really considered a bonding act since it can occur anywhere from a few minutes to a few hours after the birth. Other theories for placenta snacking include:

1. Hunger—the cow is understandably hungry and craving a high-protein post-natal snack, and a pile of placenta is conveniently close.

2. Predator avoidance—to remove any evidence of the birth so the smell doesn't attract hungry predators.

3. Instinct—no explanation; they just do it.

Baby calf poop in itself is pretty gross-looking although maybe not much different than human baby poop from a breast-fed baby. It is a dull mustard color and the consistency is runny. If, however, the calf stool starts to turn a dirty white, there is a problem. The calf has what is called "scours," a severe diarrhea that can prove fatal if left untreated. An antibiotic pill and/or shot usually take care of it.

Cows, like most outdoor-residing animals, relieve themselves any time, anywhere. They do not sniff all over the pasture like dogs sniff all over the yard to find just the right spot. They weren't designed with a "holding mechanism" like humans. You will not see a cow standing crossed-legged with a look of desperation on her face. They just let go. If some unsuspecting calf decides to eat at the rear end of the table, rather than from the side, it risks being bombarded. I related earlier about watching this happen and the calf ended up with a big, dark green cow pie on its head.

Anybody need a barf bag yet?

Have you ever seen cows standing or lying around in a pasture chewing on something? You probably assumed they just bit off some grass and were giving it a few chews and would then swallow the mouthful. That assumption was probably correct up to a point, but there is more to the process and this is where it gets gross. Those cows were chewing their cud.

Chewing Cud 101: The digestive systems of ruminants—cows, goats, sheep and antelope—are unable to produce enzymes necessary to breakdown the cellulose material of plant matter. So when a cow chews and swallows grass or hay, an alternative digestive process is set in motion whereby once the plant material hits the rumen, the first stomach of a multi-stomach system, it is regurgitated back up as cud, along with bacteria to aid in the breakdown process, to be re-chewed to become more digestible.

This is an over-simplified version of the process. At least it sounds better than cow eats grass, barfs it back up, then chews on it for awhile. My very strict and straight-laced high school home economics teacher, Mrs. Dutton (God rest her soul!), always said students chewing gum looked like cows chewing cud. Think about that the next time you put a stick of gum in your mouth! (Believe me when I say there is no gum-chewing in Heaven, not even by the Big Guy Himself. With Mrs. Dutton around, He wouldn't dare!)

Bon Appetit!

Our beloved farm pets have exhibited some pretty gross habits. Most of these habits involved animal feces or dead animal matter.

All of our Golden Retrievers have been enamored with cow manure—both eating it and rolling in it. When we had two dogs, one older and one pup, I assumed the older dog taught the pup the finer points of manure. But with Cricket, our current dog, there wasn't an older role model. She picked up the nasty habits on her own. It has to be an instinct thing!

Poop-snacking usually occurs when Cricket is out in the pasture with us on our evening walks. She makes a beeline for a cow pie, usually a fresh one, and starts nibbling. We call her off but she is usually reluctant to leave her feast. It takes a stern "Cricket, Come" command to get her attention.

Baby calf poop must be particularly delectable. Brandy and Amber both learned usually the first thing a baby calf did after it got up from napping was to poop. So they would trot up to an unsupervised sleeping calf, abruptly wake it so it jumped up, ran a few steps, stopped to poop, then continued on to find Mama, who by now was charging toward the calf at a dead run. Both dogs would have to be quick lapping up their snack.

Obviously, a diet that includes cow feces has to have some ill effect on our dogs. Fortunately, the small amount they eat doesn't cause any health issues. It will cause them to have bad breath for awhile. It also produces flatulence. Many an evening we have been sitting in the living room with one or two dogs napping on the floor beside our chairs when suddenly the most obnoxious stink imaginable—worse than the rotten egg gas we made in high school chemistry—filled the room. There was no audible warning; these were Stealth Farts! Of course, our first reaction was to accuse each other, and we both vehemently denied being the culprit. Then we looked at our beautiful, lovable Goldens and remembered: Oh yeah—the early evening poop snack was now peeling paint off our walls!

Our dogs are also quite fond of afterbirth. If the cow doesn't eat it, they will, unless we find it first and dispose of it. Even if the cow did eat it, any of our dogs would sniff out the birth spot with their bionic noses and lick the grass to be sure there were no lingering traces.

Fortunately, Cricket has not yet discovered the fine art of rolling in cow pie. Our previous dogs all reveled in a good roll in the pie. Then, they would trot up to us, wide grins on their faces, as if they were proud of this particular accomplishment and wanted to be rewarded with a big hug. They got a bath instead!

If you are still with me here and have not yet run for the bathroom, you're doing great!

Gross Dead Smelly Stuff

Dogs also seem to have an affinity for rolling in dead animal corpses—the deader, the better! Anything with a high maggot count is a particular treat. Fortunately, the corpses are usually birds or small rodents, but the smell is just as bad as that of a larger animal. If I happen to look out into the yard and see our dog look intently at something on the ground, sniff at it, drop to the ground and roll in it, I grab rubber gloves and a plastic bag and race out to confiscate the dead toy. We never throw away old bread sacks—they make great body bags. The bag is sealed, then placed in the freezer of the "beer" frig in the garage until trash day. If I try to dispose of the corpse anywhere on our acreage, that dog will use her extraordinary nose to sniff it out, retrieve it back to the yard and continue to amuse herself.

One recent evening, Cricket and I were returning from our walk in the pasture. Cricket stopped to explore something and I walked on. In a few minutes I heard thundering paws approach behind me. Cricket tore past me, then stopped and proudly pranced around with her find: a leg from a calf—a recently deceased calf. Besides being totally repugnant, it was also alarming. At this point, we didn't think we were missing any calves. I took the leg from Cricket, who looked extremely disappointed to have her new toy confiscated, carried it to the house, put it in a plastic bread sack and placed it in the morgue freezer. I told Bill about Cricket's find and we did a calf head count but weren't missing anyone. We also checked the cows that, so far as we knew, had not yet given birth. None of them appeared to have calved in the last couple of days. Bill concluded the leg came from an earlier stillborn calf. After he had skinned off the pelt, he tossed the carcass over the back fence as a treat for the predators. Apparently one of them dragged a leg about a quarter of a mile to where Cricket found it.

Skunks

If you live in the country and your dog spends time outdoors, getting maced by a skunk is unavoidable. I guarantee it. Some dogs seem to learn their lesson with one encounter. Unfortunately, we have never owned any of those dogs. I lost count of the number of times we de-skunked Amber. She would race up behind a skunk, stick her nose in its butt and take a full hit in the face. The high concentration of the defensive chemical warfare gas would sting her eyes and make her froth at the mouth, causing her to race around the yard and roll in the grass in a futile attempt to rub off the residue.

We were fortunate to find an antidote that has proven to be fairly successful in neutralizing the odor:

1 quart 3% hydrogen peroxide

¼ cup baking soda

1 teaspoon liquid soap (Soap breaks up the oils in the skunk spray)

This procedure works best when used immediately after the dog has been skunk-maced. We hose down the smelly victim to remove any surface residue. Then we mix up the above ingredients in a small bucket and, wearing rubber gloves, suds her down and keep sudsing for several minutes. Since Amber usually caught it in the face, we had to be careful with the solution because it would further irritate her eyes. I had fairly good luck tipping her head up and rubbing solution on her head, ears and nose. After a thorough sudsing, we hosed off the antidote.

Sometimes, if the skunk sensed Amber was closing in, it would mercifully fire just a warning shot. The cleanup only involved her head and shoulders so half of the solution usually did the trick.

This antidote works fairly well but it's not a miracle cure. There may be traces of lingering odor that usually disappear in a couple of days.

One summer evening during hay season, Amber attacked and attempted to clear out a nest of young skunks. The hay crew kids finished unloading the hay wagon and headed to the house to restock with water and sports drinks before returning to the meadow for another load. One of the kids and I walked out of the barn just in time to see Amber dive into a drainage tube under the driveway and back out with a small black creature in her mouth. She then proceeded to shake it vigorously. My first thought was she had one of the neighbor's kittens so I yelled "Amber, no!" and we started to run over to her. Three steps and we hit a wall of skunk odor! Amber dropped the skunk and dove for another one. We both yelled at her again. This time she dropped the skunk and very reluctantly came over to us. Whew! De-skunking was obviously going to take awhile!

I experienced an up-close-and-personal encounter of my own one evening. It occurred near the end of a three-mile training run when I was a competitive runner. I had just charged up a small hill and crested the top, when I saw a small critter waddle across the road about ten yards ahead of me. Since it was dusk, I couldn't see the critter well enough to identify it so I closed the distance to about five yards. Then I saw the white stripe. *Yikes, a skunk!* I froze. I didn't even breathe. Since the run had been fast paced, *I really needed to breathe*. The skunk waddled off into the ditch. I breathed. After about a minute, I trotted on home.

Yes, living on a farm requires a strong stomach. You just never know what you'll see, smell, step in or have to hose off the dog!

Okay, on to more pleasant topics. Hey, how about food!

HAUTE CUISINE ON THE FARM

Living Off the Land and the Lake

When I was growing up, my parents always planted a huge garden. Mom froze, canned and water-bathed the produce. I still remember the day she was canning green beans and the pressure gauge on the canner hit the red zone. She evacuated the house until the pressure dropped back into the safe zone. Scared the daylights out of us kids! But once the danger passed and we realized there would be no exciting explosion, we were kind of disappointed.

When I met Bill, he had a large garden. Remember the broccoli bouquet? Bill was raised on a farm and most of the food on the table came from the farm: meat, milk, vegetables and fruit. He also is an avid hunter and fisherman. We live about two miles from a reservoir, Lake Perry, which is teeming with catfish, crappie and white bass. Bill also fishes farm ponds in the neighborhood.

The timber on our farm is full of deer and wild turkeys so Bill doesn't have to go far to bag either one. He does most of his pheasant and quail hunting in the central part of the state where the bird population is heavier and he has permission to hunt on private property that doesn't get a lot of pressure. Although I don't care for duck, he still likes to jump ponds and the dogs love to retrieve. He just gives the ducks away to friends.

Even though we are cattle farmers, in the past we didn't eat much beef and never had any of our own butchered. However, recently this changed. After years of ordering restaurant steaks, which supposedly graded as choice but turned out to be bland and not as tender as we expected for the price, Bill became curious how his own beef would grade and taste. He consulted with an area feedlot owner who was buying our yearling calves, and also with a friend who owns a meat market in Kansas City and buys calves from the feedlot owner. They advised him most of our calves graded as choice and some even as strong choice, but not quite prime. So Bill selected one of the calves to have butchered and we split a side with his sister and her husband.

We've discovered our own beef is far superior to the restaurant beef we have eaten in the past: flavorful, juicy and tender. In fact, you won't find steak sauce in our kitchen. It would be a travesty to destroy that wonderful flavor in a flood of steak sauce. Not at my table!

Before we started eating our own beef, Bill actually preferred pork. Either one, pork or beef, creates a bit of a dietary problem for someone like me with a family history of elevated cholesterol levels. Bill's cholesterol reading is so low it's in negative number range, so he doesn't have to be concerned. I do. His metabolism operates in overdrive most of the time so he doesn't have to be concerned about gaining weight. I do. He can play fast and loose with dietary indiscretions. I can't. *Dang!*

Bill was an accomplished cook when we met. The Law of the Kitchen is: you kill, you clean, you cook! And he does all three quite willingly. In fact, we split the cooking duties half and half. With two deep freezers full of fish, pheasant, quail, venison and garden produce, we do not eat out very often. For us, the cost of eating out is a line item in the entertainment budget, not the food budget. Dining out at a restaurant with wait staff, multi-page menus and a wine list containing wine in bottles with real corks, is an occasion usually done in conjunction with an event and with friends.

Even then, we rarely go to four-star restaurants; the ones where the sommelier ceremoniously uncorks the wine at the table and you are expected to perform the wine-acceptance ritual: sniffing the cork, swirling the wine around in the glass, sticking your nose halfway into the glass to whiff the bouquet of the wine and finally, taking a sip to experience the bouquet. We toured wineries in Sonoma Valley, California, and I can give a fairly believable impression that I know what I'm doing when performing this ritual. I just can't do it during haying season because then the wine bouquet is, "essences of brome and fescue enhanced by crisp tones of alfalfa with hints of machine grease and sweat, followed by a really weird finish!"

To Die For...Literally?

Bill introduced me to a highly anticipated rite of spring in the hunter-gatherer world: hunting morel mushrooms. This is truly a back-to-nature experience. Morels are found in heavy timber and along creek and river banks in mid-spring. Moderately wet weather followed by a few days of warm temperatures will coax these little delicacies from the ground. Hunting them involves trekking through timber; getting tangled up in thorn bushes; risking up close and personal encounters with snakes, venomous or otherwise; wandering into a marshy area you didn't know was there; and having ticks hitch-hike back to the house on your body while sucking up your blood. Definitely an adventure, but bringing home a plastic bread sack full is worth it! Our favorite springtime meal is fresh pan-fried crappie, home-grown asparagus, and sautéed morel mushrooms.

Early in our relationship, Bill took me morel hunting at his folks' farm southeast of Topeka. This City Girl showed up in white shorts, a stretchy little tee shirt and a brand new pair of dressy tennis shoes. The timber wildlife would be absolutely dazzled! Due to my inappropriate morel-hunting attire, I didn't venture into any dense timber; I stayed mostly along the edge of the trees. But I did get my dressy tennies muddy crossing a creek. A misstep off a rock took care of both the newness and the dressiness.

We found a few morels and went back to Bill's farm. He cooked them for supper, along with fresh crappie and asparagus. While he was cooking, I had a horrifying thought: *Didn't people die from eating poisonous mushrooms gathered out in the timber?* My recollection was that some were okay but others were lethal and some people didn't recognize the difference until it was too late. Bill seemed knowledgeable about what to look for; he had hunted and eaten morels previously. And they smelled so good, sautéing in butter and a few herbs. How could they possibly kill me?

Bill filled the plates and we sat down to eat. I poked at a morel with my fork, then apprehensively stabbed and put it my mouth. *Ummmm—to die for...*literally? I swallowed, then sampled the crappie and asparagus. More *ummmm's.* Soon, my plate was empty and I was still alive—no excruciating stomach cramps and no barfing up my socks. So far, so good!

When I went to bed that night my last thought was, "Will I wake up in the morning?"

I did, and I've been eating morels ever since!

Fashionista at the Fur Harvesters' Supper

In those early years, Bill introduced me to another food adventure I wasn't quite so impressed with, a fur harvesters' supper. Fur harvesters trap little furry animals to skin and then sell the pelts. This practice wasn't new to me; my brother did it as one of his many money-making projects as a teenager. What I didn't know was fur harvesters actually had an organization, and the local unit marked the end of trapping season with a supper featuring a menu of the meat from these little furry animals: beaver, raccoon, opossum, muskrat and groundhog. Mental picture: Granny in the 1960's sitcom, *The Beverly Hillbillies,* standing at her stove stirring a big pot of boiled possum victuals.

Bill was taking me to a supper where I would eat...what? Cream of Critter Soup? Raccoon Ragout? Braised Beaver? Surely, some other little town in the area was having a chili supper or fish fry we could attend. Oh well, hopefully the menu included side dishes and dessert.

When we arrived at the community building and walked inside, we were met with a tantalizing aroma, which was a mixture of barbecue, roasted meat and something smoked. This might be okay after all!

People eagerly headed toward the start of the buffet line chatting, laughing, and exchanging trapping tales of yore. We joined the throng, grabbed paper plates, napkins and plastic flatware, and then proceeded to the table displaying the featured fare. The meats were prepared a variety of ways and each dish was labeled. I read the names and gamely forked a couple of bites of each type of animal, uh, I mean *meat* onto my plate: Groundhog Baked in Savory Brown Gravy, Pulled Possum in Barbecue Sauce, Braised Muskrat, Smoked Raccoon and Fricasseed Beaver. I moved on to the next table and heaved a sigh of relief. (Hopefully, that was all I would heave.) It contained vegetable casseroles, bowls of salads and an array of breads and rolls. The last table was loaded with desserts. At least I wouldn't starve.

We found a couple of empty seats at a table and sat down. I put on my friendly "Hi-I'm-June-and-I-don't-know-a soul-here" smile, which immediately froze on my face. The gal sitting across from me was decked out in a vest and matching cowgirl hat fashioned out of small squares of cut-up colored plastic jugs—bleach, laundry detergent, fabric softener, dish washing detergent, probably even motor oil and transmission fluid—that were all crocheted together.

She wore the vest over a plaid western-style shirt of coordinating colors. Where did she find a white-maroon-blue-yellow-red-green-orange-black plaid shirt? The bottom half of her outfit consisted of blue jeans and a leather belt fastened with a big engraved buckle. I assumed her name was hand-tooled across the back of the belt. Curious about what she was wearing on her feet, in all probability *not* penny loafers, I "accidentally" dropped my napkin on the floor, giving me an excuse to duck under the table. No surprise, she was wearing cowgirl boots.

By contrast, I was wearing City Girl "preppy": dark tailored slacks, muted pastel-striped button-down shirt, color-coordinated with a pull-over v-neck sweater and, of course, penny loafers. We were polar opposites in the world of fashion.

Then I looked around the room. The fashion statement was "small town Saturday night": a clean pair of jeans or bib overalls; a denim, chambray or plaid flannel shirt or a sweatshirt proclaiming the wearer's allegiance to KU, K-State or the Kansas City Chiefs; cowboy/girl boots or lace-up work boots; cowboy/girl hat or a cap announcing the wearer's preference for Ford, Chevy or John Deere. There was even a guy wearing a Davy Crockett-type coonskin cap complete with the striped tail hanging down in the back.

Oscar Wilde once defined *fashionable* as "What one wears himself; what is *unfashionable* is what other people wear." Well, Oscar obviously never attended a fur harvesters' supper dressed in citified preppy. I was definitely *not* the *fashionista* at this shindig.

In a lame attempt at damage control in case I was already labeled a city snob, I greeted the gal in the plastic jug vest. "Hi! That's a very, um, interesting outfit. Did you make it yourself?"

She proudly beamed, "Oh yeah! I designed it and cut up the plastic jugs, and Ma crocheted the squares together. We got this great idea: we're gonna set up a booth at craft fairs. These oughta sell like hotcakes!"

Since no one offered up a blessing to sanctify the critters that we were about to eat, I bowed my head and silently offered my own fervent plea: "*Pu-leeze*, God, grant me the strength to not hurl cooked wildlife all over the table and floor so I don't embarrass Bill or myself. Oh, and don't let my mother *ever* find a crochet pattern for that get-up! Amen."

Still reeling from the effects of my apparent fashion *faux pas*, I cautiously approached the chunks of meat with my fork and reminded myself to think of them as just that—meat. The groundhog was surprisingly tasty, probably because the gravy was heavily seasoned. The possum was greasy and the actual taste had mercifully drowned in a vat of *KC Masterpiece* barbecue sauce. The flavor of the raccoon was a blend of salty, spicy and smoky, but after chewing one bite for several minutes, I wondered if someone had mistakenly smoked the pelt instead of the meat. The muskrat had a strong flavor I didn't like and couldn't choke down. Where's a good robust merlot when you really need one? I would have settled for a cheap burgundy.

My pick for best-in-show of the fur harvesters' supper went to the fricasseed beaver. It was flavorful, fork-tender, and reminded me of the roast beef my grandmother made using dry onion soup mix.

I was herding the pack of former little furry animals around my plate and trying to keep up with the table chit-chat when suddenly Annie-Oakley-of-the-plastic-jug-ensemble loudly smacked her lips and proclaimed, "Mmm-mmm! That's sure good 'rat!"

Time to go find the dessert table.

REUSE, RECYCLE, REPURPOSE
THE FARMER'S SURVIVAL TRILOGY

Dristan bottles—hundreds of them. I had never seen so many of those little brown bottles, which formerly contained a popular antihistamine and decongestant, even on drugstore shelves! Now I understood Bill's obsession with squirreling away every container with a lid.

The *Dristan* Revelation hit me when Bill's family gathered together to spend several weekends cleaning out the farm Bill's great-great-grandfather Hilbert homesteaded in 1857. (We have the original land grant document signed by President James Buchanan secured in our safe deposit box.) My thought as we cleaned out the house, huge barn, garage, chicken house, brooder house, old railroad boxcar, machine storage shed, sheep shed and numerous other sheds, the specific purposes of which I have forgotten: *My word! Did these people ever throw away anything?!* The obvious answer was "No!"

If you have parents or grandparents who lived through the Depression of the 1930's, you may have heard stories of the personal deprivation and extreme measures people undertook just to survive. The words "recycle" and "repurpose" were decades away from being coined, but the concept of reusing an item or stretching an item, such as food, to get the greatest possible usage out of it was imperative for basic living. Nothing was disposed of until it was completely worn out. Such was the case on the Hilbert farm.

Meanwhile, back at the farm...The womenfolk were cleaning out the house and the menfok were emptying the out buildings. At one point, as I hauled yet another garbage bag out of the house, I wandered over to one of the miscellaneous sheds to check on the progress. Bill's three nephews-in-law were literally shoveling debris out of the shed and pitching it into the bed of a pickup. I ventured over to the pickup to check out the debris. What I saw were containers of every shape, size, and material, both with and without lids: tin cans with labels, rusty tin cans without labels; some plastic containers but not many since part of the debris predated the invention of plastics; glass jars and bottles of every size, shape and color. The contents of these containers: every size of nail, screw, bolt, nut, washer and fence staple; unidentifiable powders, liquids, pastes and greasy-looking stuff.

As I surveyed the debris, I saw what appeared to be hundreds of little brown glass bottles. I picked up one and looked at it. The faded remnants of the label indicated this was a *Dristan* bottle. That's when the *Dristan* Revelation hit me and, to this day, is still indelibly etched in my brain. Now I understood Bill's obsession with saving and reusing otherwise disposable containers: it was a component of his family's gene pool. I assumed their gene pool was also stored in some type of repurposed container with a lid.

Still reeling from the *Dristan* Revelation, I was further assaulted by a terrifying premonition: At some time in the future, this estate disposal would happen at our farm as a group of family descendents repeated this very same chore. *Oh...my...word!!*

To be honest, I admit this hoarding obsession was also part of my genetics. My parents both grew up on farms during the Depression. As the oldest offspring in my family, I inherited a substantial portion of this repurpose/reuse trait. I am my mother's daughter; I can save plastic containers and plastic bags with the best of them. I have one whole kitchen cupboard dedicated for storage of not only Tupperware and Rubbermaid containers, but also margarine, whipped topping, cottage cheese, cream cheese, sour cream, yogurt (the 24-ounce size, not the small 6-ounce size—I'm not *that* neurotic!) and miscellaneous mystery containers. I even have a plastic tote to store the lids so they aren't scattered all over the cupboard.

But, come on, there is a limit! In a desperate effort to keep the house and outbuildings from being overrun with plastic containers, when I empty one and determine we have an ample supply of that particular container, I make it disappear. I have a top-secret hiding place that serves as a temporary repository until I can get to the recycle bins. That repository is, you guessed it, a large container with a lid!

BOVINE DATING AND MATING HABITS

CAUTION: Rated R—May contain sexually explicit material not suitable for city-dwelling kids. Farm kids are exempt; they know all about farm sex.

Romancing the Cow

When Bill started his cow-calf operation, he eased into it by purchasing 13 pregnant cows from a neighbor. The next stage in the progression was to breed our own cows, then calve them out. Breeding cows required a bull: either a borrowed bull or Rent-A-Bull. At that point in time, purchasing a bull was not an option financially. So we rented one.

Once we had a bull in the pasture, the inevitable occurred: he had sex with our cows.

With this progression to the next stage of the cow-calf operation, I learned cattle do not have sex, nor do they make love, make whoopee or do the big nasty. They *breed*. A cow does not get laid; she gets bred. Not to be confused with getting bread for getting laid—that doesn't happen either. Nor have I heard the technical term *intercourse* used to describe the bovine breeding process. As with most animals, breeding is an unemotional natural instinct with a purpose: propagation of the species. This is another process managed by Madam Nature, uh, I mean Mother Nature.

Now, that's just too boring for words, particularly *my* words. So here's my perspective on *Bovine Dating and Mating*.

Bovine dating and courtship are relatively short in duration compared to the human version, usually lasting anywhere from a couple of minutes for a quick "wham bam, thank you ma'am" with a hussy, to several hours of serious persuasion in pursuit of a cow playing hard-to-get. If the target cow is in heat but spurns the bull's advances, he follows her around the pasture, his nose never far from the come-hither aroma wafting from her rear-end, all the while pleading his case until she relents and permits him to sire her next calf.

At times during a breeding season, Bill has been gone one or two nights a week on work-related trips. On those evenings, when the dog and I went for our walk in the pasture I searched for the bull and made note of the ear tag number of the cow he was "dating" that evening. Later, Bill called to get the "Date of the Day" report. My date-watch instructions also included writing the ear tag number of the cow on the current day of the wall calendar in the kitchen so Bill could project the probable date of the blessed event.

Cattle do not mate for life. In most cases, they don't even mate for one day. A bull "loves 'em and leaves 'em," preferring to play the field, or pasture. If several cows come in heat at the same time, that bull is one happy stud!

One of our most memorable Rent-A-Bulls was a huge, silver/gray-colored Charolais cross—a majestic specimen with impressive-looking "breeding credentials." Those mountain oysters could have fed a third-world country! When Bill backed the stock trailer up to the loading chute and opened the back gate, that bull barreled into the corral like a sailor hitting a brothel after a year at sea.

The air was charged with undulating waves of breathless sexual anticipation. Immediately, the bull's mating radar guided him unerringly to a cow nervously awaiting what nature had preordained and what she accepted as her destiny. The great stud rose up behind her and mounted. He thrust himself into her and jack-hammered toward the ultimate moment of release. With a great roar, he spilled his seed into...

Oops—sorry! I jumped genres from farm experience memoir to steamy bovine bodice-ripper romance. Better cool off here or this book will end up in the "18 and Over" room of a seedy bookstore.

The bull performed his predestined duty and immediately scoped out another target, then another. Kind of like speed dating but the bovine version would most likely be referred to as speed breeding. Once his mating radar ceased registering heated blips, he staggered over to a quiet corner of the corral, wearily slumped down and lit up a Marlboro. Just kidding about the Marlboro!

During the time we rented this bull, we called him "The Silver Bullet."

When a bull has serviced all the eligible cows in his domain, he gets bored. And a horny, bored bull can do a lot of damage. He can wreck fences, pillage pastures, bellow bull smack and beat up on a neighbor's bull, and rape pre-debutante heifers (remember Jailbait?). If the marauding bull is genetically predisposed to sire large calves, the risk factor of difficult first-calf heifer births increases. On two occasions, a neighbor's bull jumped the fence and wreaked havoc with our planned parenthood schedule. The result was a few of our fall calves were born in April (remember Peggy Sue?).

We now own two bulls. One is genetically-engineered to be compatible with first-calf heifers. To understand this concept, think of it from the perspective of the father of a teenage girl: "This is the guy I would be most comfortable with my daughter losing her virginity to." Or maybe not. The other bull has genetics to produce larger calves that will gain weight quickly. When these bulls have fulfilled their duty with our own stock, Bill loans them out to neighbors. This is how we avoid "bored bull syndrome."

Compared to the human male, the breeding lifespan of a bull is exceptionally short, approximately five to seven years, due to the frequency and intensity of the breeding. Average breeding frequency is 30 cows in 60 days. Some cattle operations do both spring and fall calving, so have two breeding seasons. Even a randy bull can only perform just so long before he needs a little R&R. Once a bull starts shooting blanks, his stud-duty days are over and he's headed for the afterlife as a Big Mac.

Love Potion No. 9*

On one bovine sex voyeurism assignment, I was derelict in my watch duties. Bill was in Wichita in early December attending the Kansas Livestock Association annual meeting. Most of our cattle had been transported to their winter quarters 30 miles away, except for seven heifers from last year's crop that Bill kept to add to our herd and breed as first-calf heifers. He wanted to monitor the breeding process to be sure they all got bred, and he wanted the project completed in two to four weeks. To make this happen would require manipulation of the heifers' estrous cycles, called *estrous synchronization*. To induce this synchronization would require injection of a chemical I like to think of as *Love Potion No. 9*.

Estrous Synchronization 101 – A reproductive management tool used to manipulate the bovine estrous cycle, i.e. chemically induce a heifer or cow to come in heat so she can be bred. The chemical is a manufactured version of

the natural hormone prostaglandin. There are various reasons for using this planned parenthood tool:
1. It forces cows to cycle in preparation for artificial insemination.
2. In the natural breeding process, cows conceiving early in the season produce calves which are larger when weaned, so weigh more when sold; ergo, worth more money.
3. Replacement heifers from early calving cows will be older for their first breeding season, therefore more likely to stay bred and less likely to have birth complications.

Whatever the reason, the bottom line is economic benefit.

So while Bill was in Wichita, I was in charge of the "Date of the Day" watch. My instructions were to check for breeding activity before I left in the morning for my city job, and when I returned home in the evening. Apparently, I didn't hear the morning part, and I also failed to grasp the critical nature of the assignment. On Thursday, I took a day of vacation from work which began with a dental appointment to replace a broken crown. From there I went to the hospital to lend moral support to a friend having outpatient surgery, then ran several errands and went home.

Bill had parked the mini-truck in the garage and left a bucket of grain in the back for me to feed the heifers and bull. Cricket and I jumped in the truck and I started the engine. As soon as the critters heard that sound, they dropped whatever they were doing and stampeded to the feed bunk, a bovine version of the Pavlov theory at work. Consequently, I didn't see who the bull was romancing. Note to Self: Next time check for hanky-panky activity *before* starting the truck.

Later in the evening, Bill called for the "Date of the Day" report. I sheepishly admitted my mistake, the result of which there was nothing to report. He took it fairly well, then asked, "What about this morning?"

"This morning?" I parroted.

"Yeah, this morning. All you had to do was look through the binoculars out the kitchen window. You didn't even have to go outside." Duly chastised, I promised to be a better bovine sexual activity voyeur.

Friday morning didn't start for me until around 8:00 a.m. I let Cricket outside to get the paper and looked out at the pasture. The heifers and the bull were crowded around the bale feeder having breakfast. If there had been any morning sex, I missed it

By the time I read the paper and drank a cup of coffee, everyone was headed toward the pond to wash down their breakfast hay. I checked the thermometer outside the kitchen window, 22 degrees. I grabbed the binoculars and focused in on the pond. It was iced over. The sky was overcast so the ice wouldn't melt anytime soon. I bundled up, told Cricket we were going for a ride, coaxed the cold-blooded little truck to start and set off to chop ice.

The first stop was the barn to find an axe and sharp-shooter, a shovel with a long, narrow blade. The ice on the pond wasn't thick so I walked along the edge, stabbing holes using the sharp-shooter, then scooped up the pieces of ice and tossed them up on the bank. I was relieved not to have to use the axe. Me wielding an axe has "disaster" written all over it.

When I was satisfied the hole was big enough to slake the thirst of seven heifers plus the bull, I loaded up the tools and headed to the barn. There was a stock tank full of water near the corral gate that had a thick layer of ice on it, but I was able to punch through with the sharp-shooter and postpone any disaster involving the axe for another day.

I was feeling pretty proud of myself for taking the initiative to go out and chop ice. Hey, if nothing else, I might have earned some redemption points to offset yesterday's blunders.

The rest of the morning was devoted to my bovine voyeurism duties. I was determined not to screw this up again—pun absolutely intended. As it turned out, there was nothing to watch; none of the heifers were in heat. I got excited once (No, not *that* kind of excited!) when the bull sniffed at one heifer's tail. But, after a couple of whiffs, he moved on to a different heifer. Nothing turned him on there either, so he tried another one with same result. Unable to score any action, he moseyed around for awhile then lay down.

Late in the morning, the phone rang. I listened as the caller ID announced Bill's cell number, then picked up the receiver and proudly proclaimed, "I'm wearing the binoculars around my neck while I do housework!" He chuckled then told me I could back off on the date watch. In talking with other cattlemen at the meeting, he learned that sometimes, when heifers have been treated to jump start the first estrous cycle, the result is a "false heat" and they may not stay bred. Estrous synchronization is not an exact science. Besides, the chemical is only active for five to seven days and we were at the tail end of the interval.

The next week, Bill administered *Love Potion No. 9* again. On Sunday, he was going to be gone for a few hours hauling home recently purchased bales of hay. On his way out the door he tossed back, "Please keep an eye on the bull and heifers."

I was already deep into mundane multi-tasking: laundry in the washer, laundry in the dryer, bed to make up with clean sheets, cookies in the oven, cookie-baking paraphernalia piled next to the sink, two bathrooms to clean, floors and furniture to vacuum. Maybe a bovine soap opera was just what I needed to add a little spark to my day.

As I pulled the last batch of cookies out of the oven I glanced out the kitchen window and saw the bull rise and mount one of the all-black heifers. Slamming the baking sheet down on the cooling rack, I grabbed the binoculars and zoomed in. The ear tag number was barely visible, but the first digit looked like a "4." *Dang!* We had two identical black heifers with numbers beginning with 4: #41 and #47. So which one was it? Still carrying the binoculars, I grabbed a coat, ran outside and took up a position in the yard with no obstructions to block my voyeur viewing pleasure.

The heifer was being coy and walked away from the bull, obviously playing hard-to-breed. Her head was turned away from me so I couldn't see her ear tag. She walked around for a few moments then looked toward me. The tag number was #47. I ran back in the house and scrawled the number on the wall calendar.

I looked out the window just in time to see the bull make another attempt to breed her. She walked away again—the little tease!—with the bull closely following, reveling in the *Eau de Siren Song* fragrance that wafted from the retreating double rump roasts. The bull didn't appear to be interested in anyone else in his heifer harem, so apparently she was the only one in heat. He would pursue #47 until he scored, even if it took all day.

Having duly recorded the tag number, my job was finished. My bovine soap opera break—*The Young and the Restless* or *The Bold and the Beautiful*, take your pick, either one applied—was over so I resumed the mundane household chores.

**Love Potion No. 9* (1959) by Jerry Leiber and Mike Stoller.

"EE-I-EE-I-O"
A LITTLE COUNTRY MUSIC

For many years I wouldn't admit it, but country music and I go way back to my potty training days. Sitting on my potty chair belting out "EE-I-EE-I-O" helped pass the time until the much-anticipated tinkle-tinkle of liquid hitting metal occurred. Gospel music was also part of my potty chair repertoire. My toddler rendition of "Jesus Loves Me" was sung with quiet melodic reverence. In fact, gospel must have been my forte because my mother requested it often!

So, music has been a large part of my life for, well, most of my life. Somewhere in the family photo albums there is a picture of me at about three years of age, standing at eye level with the keyboard of my Grandma Michaels' (paternal grandmother) upright piano, little fingers playing some unknown melody. I also loved to sit beside Grandma on the bench while she played and sang funny little songs such as "Three Little Fishies," or "Mairzy Doats."

When I was eight years old, my parents decided I was old enough to take piano lessons. Grandma gave us her piano, Dad and a crew of his friends moved it from the farm to our house and my lessons commenced immediately after school let out for the summer.

One of my earliest performance gigs occurred in a rural venue. I was the featured piano soloist for the Christmas program at the grange where my Granddad and Grandma Taber (maternal grandparents) were members. Okay, so it wasn't Carnegie Hall. It was the Fairplain Grange Hall and, admittedly, I was the *only* piano soloist.

My selection was "We Three Kings," which, nine-year-old child prodigy I was in *my* mind, I considered to be quite sophisticated. No sissy "Jingle Bells" for this virtuoso! My performance was flawless. I struck the last chord, paused, rose and bowed to enthusiastic applause! My grandparents were beaming; they were proud of me. I beamed back, happy that I could bring those wide smiles to their faces. I was to make several encore appearances in future years.

By the time I entered high school, my musical talent extended to playing clarinet in the band and piano accompanist to vocal and instrumental ensembles and soloists. Again, my music led me to a rural-related venue when friends in 4-H asked me to accompany their trumpet trio and one of the members also performed a solo. They all won purple ribbons at County 4-H Day and advanced to the Regionals where, again, they all took top honors.

My musical endeavors led to an appreciation of most genres of music. My piano studies were predominantly classical music. School band and choir were a mixed-bag of genres which, at one spring concert, included country and western music. There was an up-and-coming young country performer at my high school. He produced a segment for the concert featuring the vocal ensemble singing country songs to his guitar accompaniment and one of my classmates doing a Johnny Cash impression. It was different from anything we had ever done and the audience loved it!

For about the next decade, my musical preference was pop music on the radio. As a confirmed City Girl, I wouldn't be caught dead listening to a twangy country music station! Then, along came Bill. While he did like pop music, he liked country equally as well. Since we both loved to dance, we went out to a local night spot that featured a country/rock band. We two-stepped, jitterbugged, cotton-eye joed and slow danced the nights away and had a great time. But I still preferred pop tunes on my car radio.

Gradually, I outgrew contemporary pop music. So I switched my radio dial to "golden oldies" from the 1950's and 60's. I jitterbugged, twisted, strolled and watusied my way to and from work. Then the radio station was sold and switched program formats, crashing my mobile toga parties, beach bashes and sock-hops. Once again, I was radio-dial surfing.

Author's Note: For those of you thinking, "Good grief, woman! Why didn't you buy some cassette tapes so you can choose what type of music you listen to during the work commute!": I preferred to listen to the radio, especially in the mornings, to get the latest news and warnings of any traffic snarls to avoid.

The lettering on my radio "seek" and "scan" buttons was nearly worn off when I finally found some decent commuting music. The song playing wasn't familiar to me, but it was a snappy tune with a good beat. A female was singing about coming home after a hard day at work. I could certainly identify with her there! When the song finished, the disc jockey came on and identified the song as "Honey, I'm Home" by Shania Twain on "your favorite country station, KXYZ." Huh? Country? It didn't sound like country—no twang, no daddy in prison, no "Tears in my Beer," no "D-I-V-O-R-C-E."

I listened for a few days and heard more songs by Shania, as well as Brooks & Dunn doing the "Boot-Scootin' Boogey," Faith Hill and Tim McGraw singing love song duets that sent steam pouring out of my speakers, and Garth Brooks hanging out with his friends in low places. I wasn't yet ready to call it *great* music, but it had good beat and lyrics.

But it was *country!* If Bill found out, I'd never live it down, especially after having been so vocal in my distaste for it and refusing to listen to it on the radio when we traveled. So I became a closet country music fan on the commute to and from work. But upon arriving home, I *always and without fail* switched the radio to a pop station. I couldn't take a chance on Bill getting in my car to back it out of the garage for whatever reason, and hearing country music when he turned the key in the ignition.

This secret life went on for several weeks. Knowing my luck was probably running out, I considered just admitting my musical defection, letting Bill have his fun teasing me about it, then getting on with my life listening to country music.

Then, one evening as I was watching TV, a commercial came on announcing the upcoming CMA (Country Music Association) awards. In past years, Bill would watch the awards show and I would leave and go read a book in another room. But as I watched the commercial, an ingenuous plan hit me: *Operation Shock and Awe.* If all went as planned, Bill would be so shocked and awed he would forget to ridicule me. Perfect! I just love doing this stuff!

On the evening of the awards show Bill had a commitment after work and would not arrive home until after the show started. Even more perfect! I set the scene and cranked up the TV volume so he would hear it when he walked in the back door. Shortly after 7:00 I saw his truck drive in. A few minutes later I heard the back door open and then *"What the...!!"* He walked into the living room and found me dressed in appropriate country attire of faded blue jeans and chambray shirt, sitting in my recliner with a long-neck beer in my hand, watching the CMA's and singing along with the performer. His jaw dropped—the *shock* of the plan. He looked at the TV, then at me and closed his mouth while a look of wonderment crossed his face—the *awe* of the plan. Then he grinned. "Wow, dear! This *is* a surprise!" We enjoyed the rest of the show and a couple more long-necks together.

As country sensation Alan Jackson put it, "She's Gone Country!"

WHEN THE LIGHTS GO OUT IN THE COUNTRY

Doesn't matter where you live, city or country, electrical outages are mighty inconvenient and uncomfortable. Extended outages can become costly due to food spoilage in refrigerators and freezers or even dangerous in seasons of extreme cold or hot temperatures. For farmers, power outages in the early spring can mean the heat lamp used in the brooder house to keep baby chicks warm goes out and the chicks are in danger of freezing. A power outage in a dairy operation means electric milking machines don't work, and the herd must be milked by hand. For hog farmers, an extended outage in the summer means the air conditioning in the farrowing houses goes out, and sows and baby pigs can die of heat stroke. Most farmers have gas-powered generators to use as backup power during outages. They can't afford not to have an alternative power source.

My first experience with a power outage in the country occurred when I was a kid visiting my grandparents' farm. An early spring thunderstorm blew in and knocked out the power. I remember Granddad, Dad and Uncle Don fighting their way through the storm to the brooder house, crating up about 200 baby chicks, hauling them into the house and stacking the crates in the kitchen. We kids thought this was great! Playing in the house by candlelight was pretty cool, but now we had baby chicks in the kitchen. Even if we couldn't play with them, we could squat on the floor, look through the slats of the crates and mimic their peep-peep-peeping. We were happily delirious! Between the chick peeping and the kid peeping, our parents and grandparents were another type of delirious.

My next experience with a country power outage occurred after I met Bill. It was mid-March and I was spending the weekend at his farm near Valley Falls when an ice storm hit. As expected, the power went out. Bill had a wood stove in the living room so the house was comfortable. However, he wasn't on rural water service; his water source was a well...with an electric pump. No electricity meant no water and therefore no indoor bathroom facilities.

I'm not squeamish about peeing outdoors. I had peed *alfresco* many times at Girl Scout day camp in an outhouse which was referred to as a latrine, like the military version.

Girl Scout Version of Latrine 101: The Girl Scout latrine starts with a hole dug in the ground, hopefully of adequate depth. The throne is a five-gallon can with the bottom removed. A regular toilet seat is fastened to the top of the can. The stall is fashioned out of four stakes with gunny sacks fastened around them. A roll of real toilet paper is suspended from a holder made out of twine and a stick. The preferred reading material is the Girl Scout Handbook. It's a good opportunity to scope out which merit badges you want to earn.

Furthermore, I learned early in my travels with Bill that he detests interstate highways in favor of secondary two-lane highways. For many years, we spent our summer vacations near Steamboat Springs, Colorado. Bill's route of choice was Highway 36 across Kansas and into Colorado, connecting with Interstate 70 east of Denver. Restroom opportunities along this route in Kansas occur every 30 to 40 miles where there are towns. However, once we crossed the line into Colorado, the towns were few and far between and most didn't have viable restroom options.

The first year we traveled this route, we were on our way home and nearing one of these little towns when I requested a pit stop. I hadn't yet reached the non-negotiable stage, but it was getting close. We stopped at a Sinclair station where I had to go in and request the key to the restroom. The older guy behind the counter grumbled we had to buy ten dollars worth of gas and he would give me the key. Then, Bill grumbled because he didn't need a fill up until we reached Kansas, where he knew the gas would be cheaper. But he put in the required amount, I took the old guy the 10 dollar pee fee, he gave me the key and I trotted around the side of the building to the unisex restroom.

When I unlocked and opened the door, I gagged. Filthy doesn't begin to describe the condition of that facility. I've used cleaner outhouses! I didn't want to go in and contemplated just walking around to the back of the building and squatting since all I needed to do was pee. But I looked around and saw several houses close by so that was out of the question. Being arrested for indecent exposure and urinating in a public place in a zero-horse Colorado town had horrifying implications, not the least of which was the thought that the jail was probably no cleaner than the restroom I was facing.

Since the urge had reached the point of non-negotiable, I tiptoed into the filth pit, crouched over the ghastly toilet, peed, yanked up my clothes without wiping, and raced back out on tiptoe. I figured my hands would stay cleaner if I didn't touch the faucets or soap. Don't even ask about the pull-down cloth towel dispenser! I also didn't trust the water. There were moist towelettes in the truck I could use. This was before hand sanitizer was invented.

Since then, when traveling through eastern Colorado, we pull off the highway onto side roads for pit stops. If bushes or cornfields aren't available to provide privacy, we make sure there are no vehicles approaching, then I squat. Bill just angles the truck so he can use an open door as one wall of a make-shift stall.

So, peeing outdoors was no big deal. I just didn't care to be pelted by droplets of ice while doing it.

Meanwhile, "Pioneer Man" was setting out containers to catch frozen water for drinking, cooking and sponge-bathing. He was planning to cook up a big pot of ham and beans on the top of the woodstove. He was positively giddy with the excitement of staging his own version of *O, Pioneer*. I didn't share his level of enthusiasm.

Throughout the day, the temperature rose until the freezing rain became just rain, then finally stopped. I walked down the driveway to check the condition of the highway. No ice, just wet pavement. I called a neighbor at my condominium complex and verified there was no power outage there. So the City Girl packed up and high-tailed it back to her condo in the city and creature comforts. At that moment, my future as a farm wife was in peril.

* * *

Several years later, after we moved to the 40-acre farm, I was home alone once again when a torrential downpour, accompanied by thunder and lightning, occurred one night. Of course, the power went out. I knew enough to keep an eye on the basement since the pump wouldn't work without electricity. However, I was a little lax in my vigil and went down to the basement to find the sump hole full and water starting to inch across the basement floor.

I grabbed a couple of five-gallon buckets and, using an old aluminum pan as a dipper, filled them about half full, since I can't carry full buckets of water. As I headed for the stairs, I realized once I got beyond the light cast by the flashlight, everything would be pitch dark. Putting down one bucket, I grabbed the flashlight and raced up the stairs. Near the top, I caught one foot on a step and fell flat out onto the kitchen floor, spilling the bucket of water, flooding the kitchen and knocking the wind out of my lungs. After a few moments of recuperation, I dragged myself to my feet and then realized my whole front was soaked. I used some of the precious air that had flowed back into my lungs to heave a big *Why me!* sigh.

Retrieving the flashlight from the middle of the kitchen floor, I grabbed my now-empty bucket and went back down the stairs. The next trip up was uneventful so I went through the garage, stepped out the back door and was blasted with hard blowing rain. Oh well, I was already soaked so I tossed the water out into the yard and raced back down for another half-bucketful.

Water was coming into the basement faster than I was bailing it out. One half-bucketful per trip wasn't going to cut it. On the next trip back through the kitchen, I located another flashlight and set it up in the garage. The first one was set up in the basement to throw light on both the sump hole and the stairs. Now I could carry *two* half-bucketfuls at a time. An unpleasant image of trying to empty one of our ponds with a teaspoon entered my mind.

The deluge outside continued for almost an hour before finally letting up. The trips up and down the stairs continued until the flow of water into the basement slowed to a trickle. Finally the power came on and the sump pump kicked in. It was then I realized what could have happened had I dipped the aluminum pan into the water at the precise moment the power came back on. Compared to the ordeal I had just been through, it would have been a merciful death!

With the crisis over, now I had to deal with my flooded kitchen floor. A few minutes of sopping and wringing left the floor cleaner than it had been in ages. I peeled off my soaked clothes, tossed them in a pile in the garage and fell into bed well past midnight, dreading the vicious retaliation my muscles would inflict on me the next morning.

When Bill returned home, he researched and found a backup pump that worked without electrical power. He bought one.

* * *

A few years later, we were hit with a snow storm in mid-October that dropped eight inches of wet, heavy snow. Correction: *We* weren't hit—*I* was hit. Bill was out of state at his annual HIS meeting. Power lines were down all over northeast Kansas. The prognosis wasn't good: power would be out for several days.

Fortunately, one of our neighbors owned a big generator mounted on a trailer. He drove around the neighborhood and powered up everyone's appliances for a couple of hours, just enough to keep food in freezers and refrigerators from spoiling. The outside temperature remained cold enough so a flooded basement was not an issue.

Bill arrived home on Thursday. Friday morning, he called a rental business and snagged one of the last generators available in Topeka. Friday evening, the power came back on and he returned the rented generator the following Monday.

Shortly after that episode, Bill bought a generator. We were starting to assemble quite a collection of backup emergency equipment.

June Hilbert

OUR GOLDEN GIRLS

In addition to quiet, wide open spaces, a dusty house, sometimes exciting evening walks, gumboots, gorgeous sunrises and sunsets, and more thrilling adventures with cattle than I ever thought possible, one of the best things Bill brought to my life has been dog hair...from Golden Retrievers. Before I met him, I didn't know the breed existed, nor what lovable, intelligent, funny companions they could be. When we met, he owned two Goldens. He brought them along on our first date.

For that first date, Bill took me to dinner at the Red Lobster. When he picked me up at my condominium, he was driving an old Volkswagen bus. He opened the passenger side door and as I climbed in, I happened to glance in the backseat and there sat two dogs. I guessed this was to be a double date. He introduced them as Dusty and Ginger and explained they were Golden Retrievers. They waited patiently in the bus while we ate. The reason Bill brought them was he was going to his parents' farm southeast of Topeka after our date to spend the remainder of the weekend. His dad had three dogs so, for Dusty and Ginger, it was like a trip to the grandparents where they could romp with their cousins.

Dusty was an older dog and had come from the local animal shelter. Bill trained her to hunt and retrieve. Since she was getting older and her hunting days were limited, Bill decided to get a puppy to train and have ready to hunt when Dusty could no longer go. Tragically, my first meeting with Dusty was to be the last. Shortly after our date, she was hit and killed by a vehicle on the highway near Valley Falls where Bill lived.

Our Goldens all shared the same attributes: unconditional love, high level of intelligence, eagerness to please, excellent retriever and hunting instincts and exuberance for life. Evidence of the exuberance is they smile a lot. Yes, they really do smile.

Yet, even as our dogs shared these attributes and possessed similar personalities, we remember each one individually for a particular trait, experience or habit.

Ginger

Ginger was the ring-bearer at our wedding. The ceremony was informal and small, attended by only our parents and two close friends. It was held at the Gage Park Reinisch Rose Garden on a Friday in July at noon; and was conducted by a judge on his lunch break. Bill's best man, Ed, owned a floral shop and fashioned a big red, white and blue bow to which the rings were attached. Bill and Ed hunted together and Ed had witnessed Ginger's excellent scenting and retrieving abilities. As he tied the bow around Ginger's neck, he joked, "I hope no pheasants get up during the ceremony or those rings are gone!" The ceremony proceeded without incident.

Bill and Ginger went on many hunting trips together. When they returned home, Bill would recount for me the unbelievable retrieves she made. "I thought that bird was gone," he would say about a pheasant he had only winged, not killed. "But that excellent nose sniffed it out and she stayed with the scent until she ran it down. What a nose and what a retrieve!"

Ginger didn't just retrieve birds. She also retrieved box turtles she found in the yard. She brought them to Bill and he turned them loose in the neighbor's pasture. One summer, he suspected she was finding the same turtle over and over so he got out his red paint and put a mark on its back before he liberated it. Sure enough, in a couple of days, she had the same turtle in the yard again.

The best non-bird retrieval story was about a pheasant egg. One day, Bill noticed Ginger had something in her mouth. He commanded her to "Come," then "Leave it." She opened her mouth and deposited a pheasant egg, intact, in his hand. A good retriever has a soft mouth. You don't want your dog to leave tooth marks or chew up the birds it retrieves. Bill kept the egg warm until he had a chance to go see his folks. His dad had a setting guinea hen so they put the pheasant egg with the hen's eggs. She hatched her foster pheasant chick and raised it with her own. It was a comical sight to see that hen walking around the farmyard followed by her brood and the pheasant chick. Eventually, the pheasant learned to fly. Bill's dad saw it one morning poised on a fence post, then it took to the air and soared. That was the last he ever saw of it. The time had come for the pheasant to seek its own kind.

As Ginger entered her senior years, her hearing deteriorated and she developed arthritis in her hip joints. The desire to hunt was still as strong as ever. But when they returned home and she lay down to rest, she struggled to get up. It was gut-wrenching to watch. Sadly, her hunting days would soon be over. Time to start searching for a new pup to train.

Taffy

The criteria Bill uses when he searches for a hunting dog is:

Must be a Golden Retriever. Bill owned his first Golden when he was in the army in Germany. "Strider" was the base dog. Strider's previous owner transferred back to the States and Bill took over the care and feeding. When Bill's tour of duty was over, he left the dog to another GI. Strider loved everybody and impressed Bill with his intelligence and temperament. He planned to own another Golden at some point in the future.

1. Must be a female. Generally, females tend to be less stubborn and aggressive than males. They want to please their masters.
2. Prefers a light-colored coat to a darker one. Strictly a matter of preference.
3. At least one, preferably both, of the parents hunted. This is a key factor. Bill is a firm believer that genetics is responsible for whether or not a dog has a good nose for scents.
4. Championship bloodlines and AKC (American Kennel Club) registry of parents. Not an important factor and certainly not a reason to pay more for a dog. Our dogs are spayed so they don't have pups and we don't participate in dog shows or field trials.

As Ginger aged, Bill started watching the classified ads for Golden Retriever pups for sale. An ad appeared one day with a phone number in the area north of Topeka. Bill called and asked his main question, "Did either the dame or sire hunt?" The owner verified he owned and hunted both; the male, in particular, had an exceptional nose for scenting birds. Bill made an appointment and we went to see the pups.

We picked out a female and a couple of weeks later, brought her home. We named her Taffy. Ginger wasn't at all thrilled at being forced to share her domain with a rowdy pup but, in time, she at least tolerated Taffy.

Most retrievers love water. After all, they retrieve ducks and geese out of various bodies of water and marshes. But Taffy's encounter with water was joyous. We bought a small plastic wading pool for the dogs to cool off in on hot summer days. Taffy would run at full speed to the pool, take a flying leap and splash down in the water, huge grin on her face and throwing water everywhere! I think she was happier *in* water than out of it.

Unfortunately, Taffy graced our lives for only a few months. One morning, she heard Bill's truck and, in her excitement at the possibility of a truck ride, raced out of tall grass and between the front and back wheels. Bill took her to the vet, but her hips were broken so she was put down. Losing a beloved pet is devastating, but there are no words to describe the profound guilt and grief when you were responsible.

After the initial shock and grief subsided, Bill once again started searching for a hunting dog to replace Ginger. He called the owner of Taffy's parents to find out when there might be another litter. The guy said his wife didn't want any more pups, but he wanted just one more litter. The dame was in heat again so he sneaked the sire into her pen when his wife wasn't home. Two months later, he called us and said we could have the pick of the litter of six.

Brandy

We brought Brandy home a few days before Christmas. Again, Ginger wasn't pleased but, eventually, she came around. While Bill taught Brandy to *sit, come, stay, fetch it here,* and *leave it,* Ginger taught her little protégé to roll in cow pies and dead animals, eat calf poop, pick ears of sweet corn and eat them cob and all, eat blueberries from the bushes and heckle skunks—truly, the finer things in a dog's life. Brandy was a quick learner and she learned well!

Once our new young retriever was ready to hunt, our old one became "June's dog" and got left at home during hunting season. Bill tried to sneak his shotgun and Brandy out of the house without Ginger knowing, but it was no good. She knew, and trotted from window to window, then went to the door and begged to be let out so she could go with Bill. She *lived* to hunt and it was sad to see her disappointment at being left behind.

Bill took Ginger for one last short hunt close to home. It's critical for a good retriever to hear and obey commands. Ginger couldn't hear the commands so obeying was a moot point. As Bill said, "We hunted where Ginger wanted to hunt." They didn't bring home any birds that day; he didn't expect they would. But the grand old warrior sniffed, flushed and pursued birds for two hours, tail wagging constantly. When they arrived home, she struggled up the steps into the house. She limped to her rug in the living room and slowly lowered herself down. Her hunting days had come to an end.

As expected, Ginger's health deteriorated over the next several months. She was an extraordinary hunter and beloved member of our family. She did not deserve to suffer any longer. We made the most excruciatingly painful decision a pet owner makes and had her put down. She was the first Golden Retriever I had ever met and I'll remember her always.

We all missed Ginger, including Brandy, but she reveled in the extra attention we lavished on her. She was an enthusiastic student of her retrieving lessons and became proficient in hand signals as well as voice commands. She continued and excelled in the questionable practices she learned from Ginger. She never saw a cow pie or dead animal she didn't want to roll in.

One day as I was hanging laundry on the clothesline, I looked across the yard and saw Brandy staring at the ground, head cocked to the side like she was intently listening to something. In a few seconds, she started furiously digging. Her front paws were working so fast they were a blur. Dirt was flying everywhere. Then she abruptly stopped, and resumed the hard staring and intent listening stance. Another few seconds passed and she flew into the digging again, this time making an agitated, high-pitched whining noise. By now, I was trotting across the yard to see what was causing the commotion. As I got close to her, she jerked her head up and launched a small object through the air. It landed and she pounced on it. Once again, she jerked her head up and sent the object flying. Then she ran to it and pounced. I finally caught up to her and called her off. She was grinning from ear to ear and wagging her tail excitedly, as if to say, "Look what I found, Ma!"

I looked at the object on the ground. It was some type of rodent I had never seen before. Because if I had seen one, I would surely have remembered a rodent with human hands. Well, almost human—there was no separation between the tiny fingers. But I was definitely looking at little hands. They were even flesh-colored. The rest of the rodent was gray and furry and had a long snout. I prodded it several times with my foot to make sure it was dead. Then I picked it up by one back leg and tossed it on the roof of a small shed where Brandy couldn't get it. She camped out on the ground by the shed to make sure it didn't come to life and make a break for it.

When Bill came home, we walked out to the shed and I showed him the rodent. He identified it as a mole. I knew about moles but had never met one in person. Since they burrowed underground, I could see the advantage of having human-like hands with the fingers attached together, versus having front feet like a rat that weren't designed to move large quantities of dirt. I could picture the mole in its underground burrow, frantically digging for its life, while Brandy, the canine backhoe, tore up the earth in savage pursuit.

Brandy continued her mole patrol and found a total of 15 that spring. She decimated the mole population and we never had another problem with them while we lived at that house. Bill was kept busy filling in the ditches she dug, but was happy to be rid of the little varmints.

Brandy had a sneaky streak, especially when she was doing something she knew she wasn't supposed to do. We trained her to stay in our yard and, for the most part, she did; unless there was something so utterly delectable at the neighbors she just couldn't resist the overwhelming temptation.

The event happened late one fall after a wet, eight-inch snowstorm that knocked out power for several days. Unknown to us at the time, our neighbors had lost their deep freeze full of food during the outage. They just tossed the thawed packages out in the yard for their dogs, all the neighborhood dogs and other animals to partake of. And Brandy partook!

I happened to look out the kitchen window and saw Brandy slinking across the pasture just beyond the backyard fence. She was slinking so low it was almost a belly-crawl. She hesitated, stole a glance toward the house, then continued with the slinking belly-crawl. Aha! That guilty glance said it all: she'd been over at the neighbors. Then I saw she had something in her mouth. I watched her crawl under the gate into the backyard then trot to the garden. I quietly went outside, being careful not to slam the doors behind me. I stood out of sight around the corner of the house and watched her dig a shallow hole in the garden and drop something in. Then she pawed some dirt back over the hole.

I left my surveillance post and walked toward the garden. As soon as she saw me she looked up and crouched low. That look said it all—*Busted!* I kicked the dirt off her buried treasure and looked in the hole. I gingerly picked it up using as little of my thumb and forefinger as I could manage. It was a piece of raw meat, possibly a steak. There was discoloration but no rancid smell...yet. I held the meat in front of her face and gave her a stern "*No!*" then I took her plunder in the house and put it in a plastic bag in the freezer until trash pickup day.

A little while later I looked out the kitchen window and saw something moving through the trees down by the creek, headed east toward the neighbors. It was Brandy. She was smart enough to figure out she had a better chance of not getting caught if she used the trees for cover instead of crossing the open pasture. I went outside, walked down the fence line and waited. Soon I heard rustling in the brush on the neighbor's property, then Brandy crawled under the fence with another piece of meat in her mouth. I rushed over to her, scolded her with a few *Bad Dog's!* and confiscated her steak. She crouched down and looked appropriately contrite. The desire to please their masters is an inherent characteristic of Goldens, especially females. So it doesn't take much scolding to get the point across. However, some females, like Brandy, are strong-willed. While she may look contrite, I knew she would go right back to the meat pile. That's also an inherent characteristic, and apparently stronger than the desire to please.

We went back to the house and I told her to "Stay!" I watched her from the garage for a few minutes. She laid down in the yard, plopped her head on the ground and let out a big sigh. I felt like a mom sending her kid to a time-out.

A few minutes later, I looked out—no Brandy. Darn that dog! I raced outside and headed around the side of the house toward the backyard. There she was, in the garden, pawing dirt off something. I knew it was a piece of meat. So I watched. She picked it up and headed toward the barn. In a few minutes, she came back to the garden, went to another of her hidey holes, pawed off the dirt, picked up a piece of meat and went to the barn. She was moving her plunder to a different hiding place so I wouldn't find it. Another inherent characteristic of Goldens, high level of intelligence—sometimes too high!

Enough was enough! While the whole escapade was funny to watch, I didn't want Brandy to start eating the meat. It had some degree of spoilage and could make her sick. Then there was the discipline issue: stern scolding didn't stand a chance against the allure of raw meat. So she spent the rest of the day in the house with me until Bill came home.

When Bill arrived, we both met him at the door, pushing and shoving to be the first to state her case. I began with "Somebody's been a busy dog today!" Brandy just sat there wearing her "Welcome home, my Lord and Master!" expression of undying adoration. I related to Bill the day's saga of steak stealing and where to look for the buried booty. He found most of it, we think, and added it to the bag in the freezer.

Brandy didn't limit her food thievery to just steak; she realized the importance of a balanced diet. Ginger had taught her how to pick fresh sweet corn, another lesson well-learned. From there, Brandy expanded her fruits and vegetables menu and helped herself to the strawberries, blueberries, cantaloupe, and tomatoes. She streamlined her corn-picking technique from picking one ear at a time off the stalk to grabbing the stalk in her mouth, uprooting and dragging it to the yard. That way, she scored two or three ears in one trip to the corn patch. What a smart, efficient dog!

We lavish attention on our Goldens, but when we're busy and can't play, they entertain themselves—sometimes even constructively! Brandy ingeniously invented a game to entertain herself. The first time I watched her do this, I was amazed. She had a stick about two feet long in her mouth. Her head was turned sideways so one end of the stick was on the ground. She was pawing at something, which turned out to be one of Bill's old socks, on the ground near the end of the stick. As I watched, she worked the sock with her paw until it was wrapped around the stick like a sling. Then she grabbed the loose ends of the sock in her mouth and shook her head from side to side, swinging the stick back and forth. Thus, the game of "stick and sock" was invented.

Besides being the mole-inator, a sneaky steak thief and the most lovable and best dog in the world, Brandy learned her retrieving lessons well. Many times, after a successful hunting trip where the dog made the retrieve of the century, Bill commented, "There will never be another dog like _____!" Fill in the blank with Ginger, Brandy, Amber or Cricket. My response is usually, "You say that, but every dog you've ever trained has been better than the previous one. And that's saying something!" Brandy was no exception. Her hunting and retrieving prowess is legendary among those who have hunted with Bill.

Bill and Brandy spent countless hours flushing quail and pheasant out of wheat and milo stubble, pastures and draws. They jumped ponds together in pursuit of ducks and geese. But, as with Ginger, the inevitable occurred: Brandy started showing signs of post-hunting trip stiffness, which became progressively worse as she got older. Time to start phasing in a new hunting dog.

Amber

Finding Amber was relatively easy, thanks to a tip from a professional associate of Bill's who worked for the Nebraska Department of Agriculture. She and her family had a Golden Retriever that came from Sioux Falls, South Dakota. Their dog was everything a Golden should be and had hunting genetics. Bill called the breeder, asked his usual questions and, in a few weeks, we were off to Sioux Falls to pick up a pup.

We made a learning experience mistake with this one. We took Brandy along so the two could get acquainted on the long ride home. Bad idea! As with bringing home a new human baby when there is an only-child sibling at home, springing a puppy on an only-child dog requires the parents to finesse their family through an adjustment period.

For the trip home from Sioux Falls, we put both Brandy and the puppy, Amber, in the back of the truck, closed the tailgate and the topper door and set off. After awhile, I turned around in my seat to check on the dogs just in time to see Brandy snap at Amber, causing her to cringe and back away. Then she started to whine and cry. The poor little puppy had been taken away from her mother and siblings and put in the back of a truck where she was terrified by the roar of the road noise. Then, when she tried to cuddle up to Brandy for comfort, Brandy snapped and growled at her. Realizing we made a monumental mistake, we moved Amber up front with us. I tried to settle her on my lap but she was fidgety and whiney. I put her up on the console so she could see out and she calmed down. Eventually she laid down and fell asleep.

After that unfortunate introduction to riding in a truck, Amber was never comfortable riding in vehicles. All of our Goldens up to that point had been excited to go anywhere with Bill in his truck. Amber had to be coaxed to get in.

Brandy eventually accepted Amber as member of the family. She taught the pup all the lessons about the finer things in life that Ginger passed down to her. As expected, Amber was an eager student. She especially excelled at Skunk Heckling 101. The dog never learned to leave skunks alone. Unfortunately, the hydrogen peroxide used in our skunk odor antidote was not available in a 55-gallon drum!

While Amber was still a pup she developed an injury to one front leg caused by running too hard and too far on our evening walks. Bill took her to the Kansas State University Veterinary School of Medicine for surgery. Once she returned home, her mobility was restricted for several weeks. She either had to be leashed or in the house where we could keep an eye on her. So on weekends when we were home, we kept her in the house with us. As a result, she learned to watch TV. Her favorite shows, of course, featured animals. If we weren't watching TV, we put on the *Animal Planet* channel for her.

One evening the following winter, we were watching the Westminster Dog Show. Amber, now fully recovered from her surgery, was asleep on the floor beside my chair. She woke up, stretched, then looked at the television screen to see what was on. One of the handlers was showing a Golden Retriever. Amber jumped up, raced to the set, raised up on her hind legs so her nose was practically touching the screen, and whined and barked at the other dog. We nearly went hysterical laughing.

After Amber learned what duck hunting was all about, she had the same reaction whenever she saw and heard the *Aflac* duck. Of course, we had great fun encouraging this behavior. All we had to say was "Amber! Dog!" or "Amber! Duck!" and she would race to the television set.

Amber embraced her retriever training, as had her predecessors, with that characteristic Golden gusto. Bill trained her in hand signals and blind retrieves and she excelled at both. Once she hit a field or draw, she was a scenting, tracking, flushing, retrieving machine.

By this time, Brandy's mobility deteriorated to the point where she suffered too much pain and stiffness to continue hunting. The desire to hunt and retrieve was undiminished; she was always ready to go and would go, regardless of the consequences. But Bill knew it was time for her to retire.

Brandy was 14 years old, in people years. She would still go on evening walks with us but we shortened the distance she covered by making her "Lay down" and "Stay" a short distance from the barn while we continued on around the pasture. When we returned to her spot, she would get up and go back to the house with us. But, all too soon, she could no longer go even that short distance. Then, her appetite diminished and she lost weight. She would not eat her dog food. We have always been strict about not giving our dogs people food, but these were extenuating circumstances. One night when Bill was out of town, in desperation I baked a potato and put beef broth on it for her. She ate part of it. Before I took her to bed, I reheated it and she finished it.

We both knew the time had come. We made the decision and Bill took her to our vet's office. Dr. Rick was truly compassionate during the process. He took Bill and Brandy into a little room and he and Bill sat down. Brandy lay on the floor. They both petted her and chatted. He injected a relaxant, then a few minutes later, he mercifully ended her suffering.

Amber continued to delight and amuse us with her antics. Brandy had taught her to play "stick and sock" and it became her favorite pastime. She collected an ample supply of sticks in the area of the yard we referred to as her toy box. Some of Bill's worn out socks also appeared there. One evening after Bill finished doing yard work, he sat down on the front step to remove his boots. As he leaned forward to unlace one, Amber trotted up to him, grabbed the bill of his cap in her mouth, then trotted over to her toy box and laid down. She didn't chew on the cap, just laid there with it and grinned, as if to say, "Look what I did!"

Tragically, Amber's time with us was cut short by a freak accident on the first night at our current farm.

Amber had learned to slip her collar. The tongue of the buckle was in the last hole. The next one tighter was too tight. We either needed to punch another hole in her current collar or buy a larger one. When we weren't home, she was fastened to a long chain at the west end of the barn, which was open so she could either be outside or inside. It was mid-June and we were preparing to move from the 40-acre farm to the 160-acre farm, a monumental process. Bill was still working for the State and this was his busy season. We should have dealt with the collar but just didn't take time. Bill had a choke chain collar he used for training so he put it on her.

Moving day was on a Monday. We hired movers for the household items and friends, family and hay crew kids helped us. It was a long day but we got the house in order and were able to stay there that night.

Amber's new home when we were gone was to be an old chicken house. Bill brought over her chain from the old barn and fastened it just inside the door, which he propped open so she could be inside or outside. During that first night, a thunderstorm moved through the area with lightening and loud thunder. Amber was terrified of storms, something she may have picked up from Brandy. We were both dead to the world asleep and were barely aware of the storm.

When Bill went out to the chicken house the next morning to get Amber, he found the chain stretched as far as it would reach into the yard and the end was broken off. Amber was gone. He called and called—no response. He searched all the rooms of the chicken house, the barn and machine shed. No Amber. He came back to the house and told me Amber was gone.

I went out and looked at the chain, which was stretched out in a northwesterly direction toward our old place. We theorized she may have been frightened during the storm, broke her chain and tried to get back to her old home in the barn. Bill went over to the old place, searched the property and called. She wasn't there. He drove around the immediate area and checked with neighbors; he walked around their out buildings and called for Amber. No response.

We spent the next couple of days driving the area, knocking on doors and distributing flyers around the neighborhood. Bill posted flyers at businesses in Meriden. I called humane shelters in Topeka, Lawrence and Jefferson County. I sorrowfully admitted to the workers at the shelters that we had committed a huge sin by putting a choke chain collar on our pet. They were sympathetic and did not give me the tongue-lashing I so deserved. I almost wished they had.

We received a couple of calls from people in the area who thought they had seen a dog matching Amber's picture on the flyers. I made a trip to a humane shelter to check out a dog that looked nothing like a Golden Retriever.

Not knowing where she was or whether or not she was alive was excruciatingly painful, then on Thursday it got worse. Bill found her.

Bill went out to the chicken house and a horrible stench hit him when he walked in the door. Somewhere in his head he knew what he would find, but wasn't ready to admit it. He searched the chicken house again. At the opposite end from where Amber had been was an old manure spreader. He found her body underneath it, badly decomposed from the hot temperatures we'd had that week.

We can only guess at what happened, but think she was terrified of the storm, and in an unfamiliar place, so she struggled to get loose from the chain and sustained a fatal neck injury. She apparently crawled back into the chicken house and underneath the manure spreader.

We went through hell that week. I was numb and went about the process of unpacking boxes and organizing the house in a mechanical state. I couldn't talk to anyone. What should have been one of the most exciting times in our lives had turned into a nightmare. The grief was compounded by guilt and the combination was almost unbearable. Our beloved pet had depended on us to keep her safe and we had failed—miserably.

It's been four years since the tragedy. The grief and guilt have subsided but not completely, and that's probably a good thing. We had always considered ourselves responsible pet owners but one seemingly small lapse cost us a beloved pet. Sometimes accidents just happen, but we have committed ourselves to doing everything in our power to keep our girls safe and prevent another tragedy.

We will never again put a choke chain collar on a dog.

Cricket

We were so numb we didn't want to think about getting another dog right away. Bill doubted he would want to hunt in the fall without a companion—just too painful.

But, Bill is resilient so he began searching the internet just to "see what was out there." He found a breeder in northern Arkansas who had a four-month old female she had intended to keep and breed, but changed her mind. No, neither of the parents hunted, but both came from championship bloodlines. Bill's comment was, "At least they'll look pretty."

The owner made one comment that got Bill's attention. The woman had chickens and when the litter of pups was just starting to explore the yard, Cricket was always the first to sniff out and find the chicken poop, a testament to her scenting ability.

So, on July 4th, we met the breeder in Springfield, Missouri, fell in love with Cricket and brought her home. Once again, our home was filled with Golden joy; our family was complete.

Unlike Amber, Cricket loves to ride in any of the trucks with Bill. No coaxing necessary. If the door opens, she hops in and takes up her position riding shotgun. She also likes to ride in the bed of the mini-truck. The first fall at the new farm, Bill was still working full time and officiating football. If he wouldn't be home until late or was staying out overnight, I would come home from work, change clothes, then Cricket and I would jump in the mini and drive through the pastures, checking cows for new calves. Cricket considers the mini *her* truck and it usually doesn't leave home without her.

Like Brandy, Cricket has become a "mole dog." When we moved to our current farm, the yard was full of raised dirt pathways, indicating serious tunneling activity below ground. With her keen hearing and sense of smell, she sniffs out the little yard-wreckers and furiously digs until she nails one or it burrows so far underground she loses the scent. When she catches one, she amuses herself much the same way Brandy did: tosses it up in the air, then pounces on it when it hits the ground. The dead mole eventually ends up in a body bag in the morgue freezer, then is interred in the trash on collection day.

One of Cricket's favorite tasks is fetching the morning newspaper from the end of the driveway to the house. Bill taught her this little task after she became proficient at retrieving the training dummy. In the mornings, when he went out to her house to get her, he would go out and pick up the newspaper; then give it to her to carry to the house. Once in the house, he commanded "Leave it" and she dropped the paper into his hand. Then he gave her a treat for breakfast. She picked up on this reward thing quickly and started running out the drive to pick up the paper without prompting. Then, much to our surprise and delight, she took this task to the next level.

The second winter at the new farm, Cricket cut one of her fronts paws on a piece of thick, sharp ice when Bill was breaking ice on a pond. The cut was on the insides of two toes and required stitches. The wound was bandaged, but we suspected she would chew it off during the night so she could lick her paw. Since her bedroom was in one of the outbuildings with a dirt floor covered with straw, we knew the wound would get dirty. We decided to do something we had never done: let a dog spend the night in the house.

The following morning, Cricket woke up Bill and he let her outside and gave the command, "high on." This means "go potty." Yes, there is actually a retriever training book command for going to the bathroom. All of our Goldens were trained to "high on" and they obeyed. Impresses the heck out of people when you tell them your dog pees on command!

A little while later, Bill opened the door to let Cricket back in the house. There she lay on the front step with the morning newspaper, still in its plastic sleeve, beside her. She got up, picked up the paper in her mouth and presented it to Bill. This was apparently her way of thanking us for letting her sleep in the house.

She continues to sleep in the house except during the summer when the nights are so warm she's uncomfortable inside. Then, we take her to her house with its fenced yard. Regardless of where she sleeps, fetching the morning paper is *her* job.

* * *

I cried enough tears to fill a small stock tank when I wrote this chapter. There were joyous tears as I remembered each of our girls for the happiness they brought to our lives, and there were tears of pain and sadness as I relived those gut-wrenching moments when they left us.

Our Golden girls were well-loved and loved well. We feel incredibly blessed to have been their people.

BEYOND THE PAVEMENT

Most of us who live on gravel roads complain about the dust, the rock dings in our vehicles, frequent flat tires, potholes and mud after a gully-washer rainstorm or a melt-down of snow and ice. But the complaining is only half-hearted. In truth, we wouldn't live anywhere else.

As I turn off the highway onto the gravel road for the final stretch of my homeward commute from work, I'm eager to get home to Bill and Cricket. I'll change into my farm duds and head outside to find them. I'll get the report on new calves born that day and whether or not Bill was able to pierce the ear tag into the calf's ear before Mama ran him off. We'll head out on our evening walk and check the cows for signs of impending births.

"#164 is bagging up," will be Bill's observation. "But she probably won't calve until the weekend."

I'll walk around behind her and counter with, "But she's pooching out and I see a short stream of goop hanging out of her rear end. I'll bet it happens before the weekend." As a City Girl, never in my wildest dreams would I have imagined myself walking through a pasture assessing the likelihood of whether or not a cow would calve before the weekend.

Once the impending birth assessments are complete, we'll climb through or over the barbed wire fence, where I'll rip yet another hole in my t-shirt or jeans, and continue our walk through my "primeval timber." Maybe we'll see deer crossing our path, or wild turkeys. Windfall hickory nuts crunch under our feet as we hike to the top of a small rise. Cricket will suddenly sprint up the path, certain that this time she will catch the elusive gray squirrel before it can scamper up a tree.

Just before the path opens into a pasture, there is a small grove of pawpaw trees. In the late summer and early fall, we'll stop and check to see if the pawpaws are ripe. We've yet to find a ripe pawpaw; the timber critters get to them first. I've been told pawpaws taste somewhat like a very ripe banana, which I don't really care for. However, if we ever get lucky enough to find a ripe one, we'll cut it open, taste it, decide we don't like it, and toss the rest. Then next year, we'll repeat the pawpaw vigil, hoping to find a ripe one. For us, it's a country ritual of fall.

As we leave the timber and head west through the pasture, we are greeted by a stunning Kansas sunset. If atmospheric conditions are favorable, the western horizon will burst with a palette of my favorite colors: brilliant coral, pink, rose and lavender. I've never experienced the aurora borealis, but consider these sunsets my own customized version.

When we get back to the house, we'll sit outside to enjoy the Kansas evening and marvel at the reflective play of colors across our east pasture as the sun sets behind us.

"Land is the only thing in the world that amounts to anything, for 'tis the only thing in this world that lasts...'Tis the only thing worth working for, worth fighting for—worth dying for!" Gerald O'Hara exclaimed to Scarlett early in *Gone with the Wind*, lecturing her about the importance of the plantation, Tara, her birthright.

The first time I stood in front of our current home and looked out across the lush pastures of grazing cattle, those lines from the movie streamed through my head and I experienced an epiphany. "*This is our land!*" I understood the pride. I understood the passion. *I understood!* This land was where I belonged. There was no *city* left in the girl.

My life begins where the pavement ends.

ABOUT THE AUTHOR

June Hilbert grew up in Burlingame, Kansas, a small town southwest of Topeka, the state capital. After graduating from high school, she attended Emporia State University and Kansas State University. Indecision about her future led her to leave those hallowed halls of academia in 1974 and seek her first and only full-time job at a financial institution in Topeka.

Several years later, June met her future husband, Bill, a part-time farmer who worked full-time for the Kansas Department of Agriculture. He wooed her with a head of broccoli larger in diameter than a dinner plate. Three years later, her internship as a farm wife began.

June retired from her city job in 2012. She and Bill and their golden retriever, Cricket, live on a 160-acre farm northeast of Topeka, where they run a cow/calf operation. She is proud she can build a fire in the wood furnace without burning down the house and navigate a farm truck pulling a loaded hay trailer over field terraces without high-centering.

June claims her next-favorite gift from Bill, after the head of broccoli, was a shiny, red hay hook.

Made in the USA
San Bernardino, CA
07 November 2015